VEILED AND UNVEILED IN CHECHNYA AND DAGHESTAN

IWONA KALISZEWSKA
MACIEJ FALKOWSKI

Veiled and Unveiled in Chechnya and Daghestan

Translated from Polish by
Arthur Barys

HURST & COMPANY, LONDON

First published in the United Kingdom in 2016 by
C. Hurst & Co. (Publishers) Ltd.,
41 Great Russell Street, London, WC1B 3PL
© Iwona Kaliszewska and Maciej Falkowski, 2016
Translation © Arthur Barys, 2016
All rights reserved.
Printed in India

Distributed in the United States, Canada and Latin America by
Oxford University Press, 198 Madison Avenue, New York, NY 10016,
United States of America.

The right of Iwona Kaliszewska and Maciej Falkowski to be identified as the
author of this publication is asserted by them in accordance with the Copyright,
Designs and Patents Act, 1988.

A Cataloguing-in-Publication data record for this book
is available from the British Library.

ISBN: 978-1849045575

This book is printed using paper from registered sustainable
and managed sources.

www.hurstpublishers.com

CONTENTS

CONTENTS

PREFACE

To most Russians, the republics of Chechnya and Daghestan are culturally and politically so foreign that they might wonder if they need a visa to travel there. This book is about everyday life in these two republics, which we call Russia's 'inner abroad'. Based on a decade of fieldwork, this book shows Russia's South as a place where a new social order is slowly being introduced, away from the secular state and the watchful eyes of Kremlin officials.

Chechnya is a chiefdom of Putin's faithful ally, Ramzan Kadyrov, to whom the Kremlin granted a great degree of autonomy, which he in turn used to limit the freedoms of the Chechen people. From the perspective of the Kremlin this local warlord brought stability and peace, but he imposed gangsterism and terror on his own nation. Tortures and killings became everyday practices, directed towards alleged terrorists and political opponents. Relatives of the persecuted were left with a difficult choice: they could keep silent in the face of Kadyrov's oppression or they could emigrate to Europe in pursuit of a better life. A third alternative—increasingly popular since 2011—was to leave for jihad in the Middle East.

Daghestan is Russia's most pious republic, where village imams impose penalties on smoking and drinking, and religious heroes stand hand in hand with Soviet ones. Here, Islamic holidays are slowly substituting secular ones—with the exception of Women's Day on 8 March.

This book is about the everyday struggles of Chechen and Daghestani men and women. It is about the women who secretly date guys they met on the Internet, and the choice they make between having sex and remaining virgins. It is about the men who use Sharia law to justify their love affairs, and about the thirty-year-olds who choose to become second wives so as to keep their careers and avoid the ostracism that comes with being a single mother. The book explores how the bodies, dress and conduct of Chechen women became a matter of national interest, and why they must keep their headscarves at hand and drink champagne in hiding—and certainly not to Ramzan's health.

This book shows Chechnya and Daghestan slowly drifting away from the rest of the Russian Federation. It features the devoted followers of Sufi masters; the Wahhabis (known locally as 'devils'), who conceal their religious affiliation for fear of persecution; and young men who survived torture but were forced to commit perjury. And it features the Daghestani villagers who live in the shadow of the fame of Imam Shamil, the nineteenth-century anti-Russian resistance leader of the Caucasian War, who today remains a symbol of resistance and is commemorated along with Lenin and Stalin. The North Caucasus is a place where nostalgic accounts of life in the Soviet Union merge with dreams of a new, better life in an Islamic state—dreams many young men try to fulfill by joining the jihad in Syria and Iraq.

* * *

'Hey, Mariyat! Putin was killed today', an old man calls out to his neighbour in the Daghestani village of Chinar. He takes a few seconds to catch his breath.

'What, here? Around the corner? Not here? So why worry?' Mariyat does not look concerned.

'No, in Moscow. I saw tons of flowers and candles at the Kremlin on TV.'

'Well, so he was killed then, what can we do? Perform a circumcision and bury him quickly', Mariyat says with a wink and goes back to sweeping her front yard. She has a dinner to prepare, a kitchen to clean and prayers to prepare for. No time to worry about Putin's death. Only late in the evening does she learn that it was not Putin but rather Boris Nemtsov who had been shot dead near the Kremlin the night before, on 27 February 2015. Mariyat has hardly heard of Nemtsov. She has long been disenchanted with democracy. She has no time to worry about politics now. She wants to go to bed early, so as not to miss morning prayers.

ACKNOWLEDGEMENTS

We are indebted to all of our Daghestani friends who we met on our way and who extended their great hospitality to us, showed us dedication and patience and offered us an insight into their lives. They include: Abdurakhman Yunusov, Tania and Efendi Chutuev, Shamil Shikhaliev, Gurizada Kamalova, Elmira Kurbanova, Irina, Aleksander, Ania and Abutrab Aliverdiev, Gusein Halilulaev, Dmitry, Aleksander and Natasha Krishtopa, Isa and Patimat from Chokh, Abduljalil from Gamsutl, and many others who would prefer to remain anonymous.

Our very special appreciation and thanks are owed to Georgi Derluguian of New York University in Abu Dhabi. The publication of this book would not have been possible without his help and constant encouragement. We also express our special thanks to Bruce Grant from New York University for his careful reviewing of one of the first versions of the English-language manuscript.

This book went through many revisions. It had many critical readers who contributed greatly to it. They include colleagues from the Institute for European, Russian and Eurasian Studies at the George Washington University, Henry Hale, Maggie Paxson, Rebecca Chamberlain-Creangă and Justin Caton, as well as Kevin Tuite from the University of Montreal, Florian Mühlfried from the University of Jena, Stéphane Voell from the University of Marburg, Ieva Raubiško from the University of Oxford, Asmaa Donahue and the participants of San Francisco Writer's Grotto classes and colleagues from Sylvia Halloran's Creative Writing Workshop in Los Altos.

We owe a special thanks to colleagues and professors from the Institute of Ethnology and Cultural Anthropology, University of Warsaw: Lech Mróz, Renata Hryciuk, Iwona Kołodziejska-Degórska, Helena Patzer and Karolina

ACKNOWLEDGEMENTS

Bielenin-Lenczowska; and to colleagues from the Kaukaz.net Foundation: Magdalena Lejman, Aneta Strzemżalska and Karolina Rzemieniuk (a co-researcher between 2004 and 2009). Finally, Iwona reserves her greatest thanks for her husband Sebastian Kaliszewski for his comments on the very early versions of the manuscript.

We are also indebted to our brilliant translator, Arthur Barys. Without his professional language skills and great cultural knowledge of the region, publication of this book would not have been possible. All of our reviewers and friends have helped us to improve the manuscript but certainly none of them is responsible for any mistakes in the book.

We extend our thanks for the generous funding that was provided to Iwona by the Kościuszko Foundation in 2012, which allowed her to revise and finish the manuscript while at IERES at the George Washington University. Funds for research in Daghestan in 2009 and 2010 were also provided by grants from the Polish Ministry of Higher Education, the Institute of Ethnology and Cultural Anthropology at the University of Warsaw, and the Centre for Eastern Studies in Warsaw.

LIST OF ILLUSTRATIONS

LIST OF ILLUSTRATIONS

ABOUT THE AUTHORS

Iwona Kaliszewska is an assistant professor at the Institute of Ethnology and Cultural Anthropology, University of Warsaw. She has been researching the North Caucasus since 2004. Her most recent study focused on Islamic radicalism and everyday politics. She has authored numerous publications about the Caucasus and co-directed a documentary about a Daghestani female wrestler entitled "The Strongwoman" (2014). She is the editor and co-founder of the Kaukaz.net website and foundation, and has been traveling around Russia, Central Asia, and the Caucasus since 1999. She is currently a visiting scholar at the University of California at Berkeley.

Maciej Falkowski is a political scientist, journalist and graduate of the University of Warsaw's Institute of International Relations and the Centre for Eastern European Studies. Since 2002 he is a specialist on the Caucasus and Central Asia at the Centre for Eastern Studies, a Polish think-tank. In 2010–2013 he served as a Political Officer at the Embassy of Poland in Yerevan, Armenia. He is an author of numerous articles on the Caucasus and Central Asia, and has published in periodicals including *New Eastern Europe and Tygodnik Powszechny*. He has been traveling around the former Soviet Union since 1999.

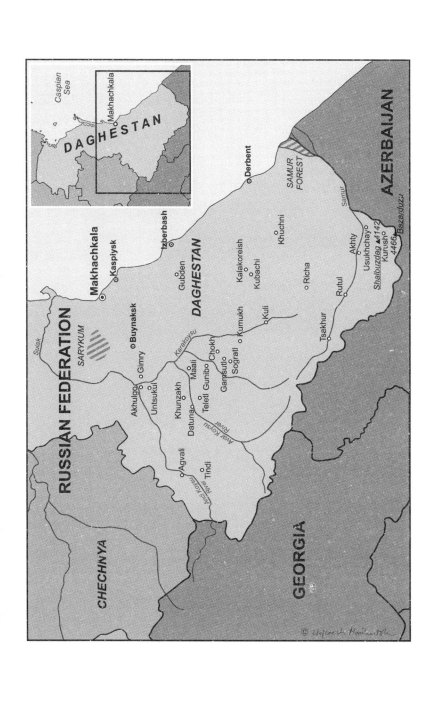

1. Tindi village, Tsumadinsky District

2. Ahkmad and Ramzan Kadyrov welcome visitors

3. The new Grozny city rising from ruins, 2010

4. Cafe "Ramzan", Grozny city

5. "Appropriate" women's outfit in Chechnya

6. Shrine near Vedeno dedicated to Kheda, mother of the Sufi master Kunta-Haji

7. Haram (sinful) at the Caspian Sea coast

8. Lenin at the Central Square in Makhachkala

9. Trendy car and a humble flat in Mahkachkala

10. Celebrating the Victory Day in Makhachkala on 9 May

11. Herding in Tsumadinsky District

12. Celebration of the opening of the new mosque in Maali, Gergebilsky District

13. Islamic University in Makhachkala

14. Celebrating Uraza Bayram in Dakhadaevsky District

15. Shrine in Gimry dedicated to Ghazi-Muhammad

16. Ghazi-Muhammad, imam of Daghestan and Chechnya (erased), local museum in Gimry

17. Chokh village, Gunibsky District

18. The sculpture of Stalin in Chokh

19. FSB (Federal Security Service) office

20. Teenage modesty, Shamilsky District

21. Lezginka dance at the wedding in Shamilsky District

22. Wedding spectators, Shamilsky District

23. The Old Town in Derbent

24. Grandmother, Kulinsky District

25. Dhikr of the women's section of Qadiriya brotherhood

26. The almost deserted village of Gamsutl, Gunibsky District

27. Godekan (village square) in Shamilsky District

28. Wedding customs in Kulinsky District

29. Presentation of the wedding gifts for the bride

30. Armoured personnel carriers on the roads of Chechnya

31. Musa's family in Koroda, Gunibsky District

32. Old and new tombstones in Gidatl

DAGHESTAN

1

ATHEISTS IN THE MOUNTAINS

'Hey boss, why didn't you pull over to say hello?!' demands the policeman, running to intercept us as we attempt a stealthy circumvention of a GAI[1] traffic checkpoint at a desolate mountain crossroads.

'We need to get you registered. Let me see your documents.'

This is par for the course in Daghestan. Our Polish passports and their Latin letters leave the officer confused. Attempting to save face in front of his staring co-workers, the sergeant leafs through the document with the air of an expert. A triumphant smile suddenly appears on his face. Peering over his shoulder, we see that he has found something familiar: an old Kazakh visa typed in Cyrillic script. The *gaishnik* (traffic policeman) impatiently searches for a pen and a scrap of paper, finally settling for a grease-stained Avar-language newspaper on to which he copies our names with a trembling hand.

'Just in case. We have to keep things in order,' he explains. We head off, trying to hitch a ride as we walk. The road winds through rocky, treeless mountains. In the distance, the Gunib plateau towers over neighbouring hills and mountain ranges. It was there that Imam Shamil surrendered to the tsar's army in 1859, marking the symbolic end of the ninety-five-year war in the Caucasus and the incorporation of Daghestan into the Russian Empire.

We are given a lift to the village of Kommuna by two cheerful young men asking with interest: 'Which part of Russia is this "Poland" located in?' The village is said to have been settled by the more enthusiastic Daghestani supporters of the then new system, who attempted to create an ideal communist community devoid of private property. They were to serve as an example to

3

neighbouring *auls* (mountainous villages), which were resisting collectivisation. The experiment failed. After the collapse of the USSR, most of the inhabitants left and the village has fallen into disrepair.

We have 7 kilometres left to go. Several brand new BMWs and Mercedes pass us by. Drivers in foreign cars rarely stop for hitchhikers in those parts. But why are there so many of them? The road leads only to Chokh and a handful of even smaller mountain villages.

A jeep approaches, but we don't try to flag it down. The car is a favourite of the local FSB (Russia's Federal Security Service, a successor of the KGB), and we'd rather avoid any trouble. The driver stops anyway. He turns out to be a friendly villager in his fifties with whom we had shared a *marshrutka* (minibus) ride to Gunib earlier that day. His Russian is very poor; he doesn't have many occasions to use it. He lives in the tiny, remote mountain village of Obokh together with a few other families, and rarely goes to town. The settlement is inaccessible to anything other than a dependable Soviet jeep, and even they can prove insufficient in the winter. He gives us a ride all the way to Chokh and drops us off at the village square. The place doesn't seem at all inviting.

* * *

'As-Salamu alaykum!'

'Wa alaykum as-salam!'

'We're from Poland.' We start to explain who we are, where we're from and why we're here, but are quickly interrupted.

'*S priyezdom!*' We are welcomed like old and long-awaited friends by the vice-principal of the village school, to whose home we were directed by a few young locals playing with their cellphones on the *godekan* (village square).

'Sit down and tell me everything.' Like every Daghestani host, Isa treats unexpected guests as old friends. 'How was your trip? You must be exhausted. How's everyone back home? Good? Praise God. Patimat, put the kettle on for tea! Bring them some food. They must be starving.'

Hospitality is one of the things visitors find most surprising and charming about Daghestan. This may be said without a hint of pathos or exaggeration. The proverbial hospitality of Poles pales in comparison to what travellers experience in this Caucasian republic. Even in countries that pride themselves on their open attitude toward guests, one can hardly expect to knock on a door, be taken in for the night, be given food and drink, and not be expected (or even allowed) to pay a penny in return. And yet that remains the norm in Daghestan.

4

It was once the custom not to ask a guest any questions during the first three days of his or her arrival. Only after that time had passed would the host enquire about a guest's name, the purpose of the visit, itinerary or the intended length of their stay, even if they were suspected of having committed a crime and of hiding from the authorities or blood revenge. Many villages had special houses set aside, often next to mosques, which offered safe haven to exiles from other *auls* or countries as well those fleeing blood revenge. The inhabitants of these homes were under the protection of the entire community, which was bound by the sacred duty of hospitality. Many of them later married local women, giving rise to new *tukkhums*, or alliances.

Daghestan was the perfect place to be if you were on the run from Interpol. Or if you happened to be one of the Chechen militants who frequently crossed the border into western Daghestan in 1999–2002 to take advantage of the local obligation of hospitality. The fighters would travel between Chechnya and the Pankisi Gorge, where they would hide from Russian forces, tend to their wounded and recuperate their strength. They were certain that the Daghestani highlanders would not give them away but would offer them food and shelter and show them the way around Russian border checkpoints.

What is the motivation behind Daghestani's extraordinary hospitality? The main reason is likely the strength and vitality of the local *adat*, the unwritten customary laws that have regulated the everyday lives of Daghestani communities for hundreds if not thousands of years. The obligation to offer shelter is one of the most important and respected laws of the *adat*. A person who refuses to offer his hospitality brings shame upon himself and suffers the scorn of the community. But Daghestanis who invite guests into their homes do not appear to do so out of obligation or fear of public ostracism. They often take genuine pleasure in fulfilling their duties as hosts and do so in a natural and unfeigned manner. Guests from far away, especially from abroad, are still rarely seen in Daghestan. To host them, spend time with them and listen to their stories can be seen as a leisure activity that brightens their otherwise mundane lives.

* * *

Isa turned out to be not only an excellent host but also an interesting conversation partner.

'I get foreigners all the time. I've had guests from England, the Netherlands ...' Judging by the stack of faded postcards and stamps Isa shows us, English travellers visited his home fifteen years ago, while Dutch guests were last seen here twenty years ago. The opening up of the Iron Curtain lured curious travellers to the Russian south in the nineties, some in the late eighties. The Chechen war and numerous kidnappings scared the foreign and local tourists off for good.

His knowledge about the history of the *aul* is admittedly enviable. He tells us about Chokh as we go for a walk around the village, which is among the oldest *aul*s in Daghestan. Its inhabitants were once known throughout the country for their love of trade. Chokh, which remained a free and unconquered *aul* until the mid-eighteenth century, once belonged to the Andalal confederation together with nineteen neighbouring settlements. In times of peace, the villages of the Andalal led their own lives, enacted their own laws and waged constant—and sometimes bloody—battles against their neighbours. But in times of war, the inhabitants of the Andalal would join forces against external threats. Holed up in their fortress-like *aul*s, the highlanders would launch attacks behind enemy lines, and usually emerge victorious.

The nineteenth-century war in the Caucasus put an end to the independence of Chokh and the entire Andalal. While neighbouring villages sided with Imam Shamil, the inhabitants of Chokh quickly joined the Russians, in the belief that there was no point resisting such a powerful enemy. Furious, Shamil had the *aul* burned down in 1842—a punishment he inflicted on many Daghestani and Chechen villages that would neither accept his rule and join the *gazavat* (holy war), nor abandon the *adat* and accept Sharia law as their only legal system. These events were documented by Mateusz Gralewski, a nineteenth-century Polish exile conscripted into the tsar's army, in *The Caucasus: Memoirs of a Twelve Year-Long Imprisonment*.

> I mentioned that the fort of Chokh was built atop the ruins of an earlier *aul* that had been destroyed by Shamil. The inhabitants of the village fought amongst themselves, some in favor of independence, others in favour of Shamil; some scattered into the mountains, while others went off to join the Moscow Infantry Regiment. Neighbouring tribes called them the *Frengs* and told the story of their recent conversion to Muhammadism.

The inhabitants of Chokh would certainly deny this claim: according to local legend, Chokh was one of the first *aul*s in central Daghestan to accept the faith of Muhammad. It is said that Islam was brought to the village by Abu Muslim, the semi-legendary, semi-historical commander of Arab military forces that reached Derbent in 652 and launched a campaign of raids and forced Islamisation in Daghestan. When Abu Muslim left Chokh, he granted rule over the *aul* to his son Osman, who is said to be the ancestor of one of the Chokh *tukkhum*s. The Arab commander gave the villagers his cloak, banner and sword, and ordered the *aul* to commemorate the annual holiday of Eid-ul-Fitr (held to mark the end of Ramadan) by having the eldest man in the *tukkhum* of Osman climb to the roof of the main mosque and brandish the sword at the neighbouring *aul* of Rugudzha, which is said to have been the last village in the area to convert to Islam. The inhabitants of Rugudzha would certainly deny this claim. Every *aul* in Daghestan has its own history.

* * *

'Chokh is an *aul* of doctors and professors,' Isa continues, showing us a pamphlet advertising an annual summer event called 'Chokh Days'. 'This was the home of many "progressive" Daghestanis: educational reformers, revolutionaries, and activists. We have always been more modern than our "backward" neighbours.'

But the latter have their own opinions about Chokh. They regard the *aul* as a village of 'communists and atheists' rather than 'doctors and professors', and speak with disdain about its inhabitants, who served the Russians while others fought alongside Shamil. They resent Chokh's support of the communist system, violently imposed by the Bolsheviks, and their fervour during the period of collectivisation (Chokhans made up the majority in the village of Kommuna). Neighbours also accuse Chokh of having abandoned Islam in favour of atheism.

There appear to be very few card-carrying communists left in Chokh. We arrived in the village on 1 May 2008. To Isa's chagrin, no one had displayed a red flag, nor had it occurred to anyone to hold a May Day march. Yet there is some evidence to support Chokh's reputation as a 'red' *aul*: the village's only mosque, located in the main square, remains unfinished and in a state of visible disrepair (despite the fact that mosques in almost every Daghestani *aul* were rebuilt in the early nineties), while the façade of the local cultural centre features a well-kept bust of Stalin.

'He wasn't an evil man,' explains Isa. 'They call him a murderer and an executioner. But things were just different back then. Name one leader who didn't kill anyone. There was no other way. Everyone here respects him, that's why they wouldn't let the statue be torn down, like they were elsewhere.'

* * *

Although Chokh happens to be an exceptional case, Soviet nostalgia and positive attitudes toward communism are hardly rare in Daghestan, even in the mountain *aul*s, where religion plays an important role in social life. These

7

parallel phenomena—the popularity of communism and the deep religiosity of most Daghestanis—remain a puzzle to researchers. One of the few attempts to solve it was made by Vladimir Bobrovnikov, a Russian orientalist who studied the social processes occurring in the remote Daghestani *aul* of Khushtada under the Soviet Union and, later, the Russian Federation. What conclusions did he reach?

According to Bobrovnikov, following a period of cruel Stalinist persecution of Islam in Daghestan, an interesting process began to occur deep in the mountains, far from the watchful eye of Moscow: the mutual permeation of Islam and communism. To all outside observers, everything looked the same as in other parts of the Soviet Union, but in reality, the Soviet state structures were a cover for Muslim institutions or even older structures based on the pre-Islamic *adat*. They were resilient enough to adapt, and de facto subjugate, the socio-political system installed by the Bolsheviks. Thus while villages appeared to run collective farms, these were in fact *jamaat*s—ancient territorial communities inhabited by free highlanders. The boundaries of the Soviet *kolkhozy* lined up with the borders of the *jamaat*s. They were led not by party chairmen or KGB officers, but by *dibir*s (imams) and councils of elders. Just as they did before the revolution, people performed the *salah* (prayer), attended home mosques, paid tithes to the imam, taught their children Arabic, read the Qur'an and resolved conflicts not on the basis of Soviet legislation, but Sharia law. With hardly anyone there to persecute them, the Daghestanis continued to practise their faith. The entire regional and village *verkhushka* (top i.e officials) would celebrate all local feasts, only to voice their support for the 'struggle against holdovers from the past' and the intensification of atheist propaganda at party congresses in Makhachkala.

Thus the inhabitants of many remote Daghestani *aul*s did not perceive the Soviet Union as an agent of severe religious oppression. They enjoyed the benefits of the stable Brezhnev years: job security, regular income, educational opportunities, summer vacations in the Crimea, cheap airfare and electricity. Why wouldn't they pine for the Soviet Union?

Above Chokh looms a 'fortress'. Surrounded by walls 3 metres tall, and illuminated by spotlights at night, the huge three-story home contrasts with the modest houses, stables and barns in the village below. We spot the *inomarki* (imported cars) that passed us on the way to Chokh parked behind the gate. 'That one belongs to our compatriot, Abusupian Kharkharov,' explains Isa. 'He was the general director of the seaport in Makhachkala and one of the richest men in Daghestan. He has four wives. I don't know how he made his fortune. That's none of my business. What matters to me is that he is a Chokh patriot. He looks out for his people. He built us a sealed road. The villagers respect him. He doesn't have a permanent residence here. He's having guests today. It looks like they're here for May Day.' There is not a hint of jealousy in Isa's voice. Had Kharkharov built his mansion in a Polish or Russian village, he would have been reviled by the locals, who might even break his windows or set fire to his house. Not in Daghestan.

Our hosts don't complain about their misfortune, though they have plenty of reasons to do so. Teachers earn a meagre wage at school and must keep cows and sheep to make ends meet. In the evening, Patimat, a Russian-language teacher at the local school, dons a pair of rubber boots, rolls up her sleeves and heads off to her barn at the edge of the village.

'Atos! Machek! Ingush!' she yells at the calves, herding them into the barn for the night.

'Ingush? Do you call any of them Chechen?' we ask. 'No, but I guess if you want we could call the new donkey Chechen,' laughs our hostess, visibly tired. There's still much work to be done. In Daghestan, the day doesn't end until the guests have had plenty to eat and drink.

'Women in the mountain *aul*s of Daghestan do not drink. Female guests from abroad are usually offered alcohol but even if one does feel like having a stiff drink, it is best to refuse the first offer to appear respectable.' That's at least what we were taught.

'Will you have a drink?' asks Patimat.

'No, I don't know. Maybe just a little ...'

'Well I'm going to have one!' she interrupts, pressing her husband to fill the glasses quicker.

We raise our toasts. 'To our guests! To our hosts! To communists and atheists!'

There aren't many orthodox Muslims in this village, unlike tomorrow's destination: the nearby *aul* of Sogratl, known by some as the 'Wahhabi village'.

2

THE BEEKEEPER-PHILOSOPHER

The *aul* of Gamsutl is perched on the top of a hill, inaccessible even to late-model Land Rovers. Inhabitants of the remote village had three ways of climbing the winding path up the hillside: on foot, on horseback or on a donkey. Although it is right above us, we can't catch a glimpse of the village. We approach each bend convinced that something awaits us just around the corner, only to discover a pile of rocks, a precipice or a dense thicket—and yet another hundred metres uphill. Whoever chose to settle in this place knew what he was doing. Any enemies, should they even figure out there were people living somewhere up in the clouds, would probably give up halfway up the hill.

The village emerges unexpectedly. We are struck by the complete, almost deathly silence. A tower or fortress of some kind looms over the *aul*. Climbing up to the top, we get a good view of the entire settlement, which stretches several hundred metres north to south. Nestled together and criss-crossed by narrow alleyways, the stone houses seem to form a single tightly packed structure. The most far-flung buildings stand at the edge of a several hundred-metre cliff. It seems as if a single stone pulled out of the foundation would send the entire home sliding into the valley below.

There is something ghastly about abandoned villages. Wandering about the empty houses, looking at the crumbling stoves, mouldy beds and old newspapers scattered in the corners, listening to the doors creaking in the wind, one can't shake the feeling of being watched, of being followed. As if someone were eying you, making sure that you didn't break anything, knock anything over or take any of the rusty pots that will never be used again. As if to be certain that everything would be left the way it was.

* * *

Perhaps someone does live here after all. We see curtains in the windows, washbasins, a bucket, a rubbish dump. But no: the door is locked. There is not a soul in sight. Then again, the outhouse with a view of the valley appears to have been used recently.

'Hello!' someone's voice suddenly breaks the silence. 'Hello! Well, don't just stand there. Come over here!' An elderly man with a broad smile waves at us from the porch of the house next door.

His beard is long and grey. He wears a baseball cap. Two rows of gold teeth fill his mouth. Is he the sole inhabitant of Gamsutl?

Abduljalil is clearly embarrassed. He had not been expecting company. He offers us a seat among the hives, swearing that the bees flying above our heads are mild-mannered and won't lay a finger, or rather a stinger, on us. Glancing at us constantly, he brews up a pot of tea. He comes across as shy and taciturn. He looks at us with a somewhat absent gaze. It is clearly difficult for him to hold a normal conversation after days of forced silence—and in Russian, no less. He reaches into the corner of the room and produces a pail. Hungry after our long hike up the hill, we greedily scrape up the last bits of honey and beeswax left on the bottom.

'I'm really sorry. That's all I have to eat. I've just run out of food and I'm going to have to go to Sogratl to pick up some supplies.' Our host slowly opens up. He says a few words and sentences here and there, as if with great effort, gradually picking up steam, and soon launches into an uninterrupted monologue, which we listen to for the next few hours. Abduljalil, it seems, wants to make up for the days, or perhaps weeks, spent in utter silence.

Abduljalil Abduljalilovich has been the sole inhabitant of Gamsutl ever since his sickly eighty-year-old neighbour was taken away to live with her relatives. A true hermit, Abduljalil doesn't even have a pet to keep him company. His only occupation and source of income—aside from the monthly pension he collects in Makhachkala—are his bees. To our great surprise, the hives are set up in his living room, which has a removable front wall, turning it into a porch with a breathtaking view of the nearby mountains in the summer.

'Bastards cut my power off a few weeks back. They said it wasn't worth the maintenance for just one person. But I don't complain. I've got my kerosene lamp, I get my lumber from the forest, and there's a spring nearby. What else could I possibly need? I sit and read and think about things. I do my cross-word puzzles. I'm too busy to be bored.'

* * *

What else could I possibly need ... A rare statement indeed. But there's nothing he is missing in his life. Bees, a kerosene lamp, a few books, a roof over his head and time to think. As you read these words, he is likely sitting on his doorstep, thinking. The beekeeper-philosopher.

* * *

The death of Gamsutl did not occur overnight. The village was still booming in the fifties. It had its own *kolkhoz* and had just been electrified. The people took their herds out to pasture in the nearby mountain valleys, just as they had done for centuries. The *aul* was still famous for its silver crafts. Then came a year when one of the village's inhabitants decided to leave. Not to visit his relatives: he decided to leave for good—to pack his belongings into trunks, lock the door of the home shared by generation upon generation of ancestors one last time, abandon the graves of his parents and leave. Another villager left the next year, and then another. The stream soon became a flood. The only ones who stayed behind were the elderly villagers who couldn't stand the thought of dying in an apartment block in Makhachkala or Khasavyurt.

But the death of Gamsutl was not brought about by dire living conditions. The *aul* had been inhabited for hundreds of years without electricity, running water and roads. The villagers ate only what they could produce with their own hands. Gamsutl only became a heap of rocks when the people saw that a different life was possible, and came to the understandable conclusion that, at least in this case, 'different' meant 'better' and 'more comfortable'. Any 'normal' person would choose a heated apartment with a gas stove, indoor plumbing and a television set over life in a stone hut on a mountaintop.

Many *auls* in Daghestan met a similar fate, but not all were abandoned 'naturally'. The history of Kalakureysh came to a brutal end. Once inhabited by descendants of the Arab Quraysh tribe (to which Muhammad himself belonged), the village was known throughout Daghestan for its madrasahs, religious schools, in which students were taught by the most renowned *alim* (Islamic legal scholar). Today, there is little left to testify to the bygone glory of Kalakureysh aside from a beautiful mosque and a cemetery with intricately carved gravestones. No one knows why this particular village was chosen while the equally famous *aul* of Kubachi, just a few kilometres away, was left alone. The logic behind the actions of the Cheka is hard to fathom. For Daghestani highlanders, the forties were a period of mass deportations of which little is known or spoken of today, and which were just as tragic as those suffered by the Chechens, Crimean Tatars and Kalmyks, who were sent to Central Asia. Daghestanis were mainly resettled within the republic: from the mountains down to the plains and west to Chechnya, where they replaced the deported natives. The NKVD (People's Commissariat for Internal Affairs, predecessor of the KGB) gave people a few hours, or sometimes days, to pack their belongings before chasing them over the mountains. Unaccustomed to life on the balmy, malaria-infested plains, many highlanders died. Some attempted to return to their ancestral homes, risking persecution and repeated deportation. The inhabitants of Khushet, a village near the Georgian border, turned out to be the most tenacious among them. They were resettled three times, and each time they returned. The authorities finally gave up and allowed them to stay, but punished them by leaving the village to fend for itself. The *aul* was the last one to be connected to the electrical grid, and was never given a proper road. To this day, the village can only be reached on foot or by horse. The path is inaccessible to any vehicle. The nearest sealed road is 32 kilometres away. When winter comes, the village is completely cut off from the rest of the world by heavy snowfall.

Most of the resettled Daghestanis eventually accepted their fate and grew accustomed to life on the plain, abandoning their mountain *auls*. But the deportees do not forget their roots. When asked about their origin, young people born in Kizlyar or Kizilyurt list the names of the villages from which their grandparents were resettled. They often marry girls whose ancestors come from the same village. They make yearly pilgrimages to their ancestral *auls*, where they visit graves, pray at the local mosque and sometimes even make minor repairs to old houses that will probably never be inhabited.

* * *

'My father was very devout. He prayed five times a day, and he knew the Qur'an and the Sunnah well. People would come to him for advice,' says Abduljalil, continuing his monologue. 'He taught me Arabic. Thanks to him, I know how to read the *ajami*.[1] He was a holy man. But I'm a fallen Muslim. I served in the army, I went to school, and then I ended up in a *psikhushka* (mental hospital) for a while ... Such is life, what can you do. I'll walk you down to Sogratl, and we can talk some more along the way.'

Clouds begin to gather overhead and it starts to drizzle. We head off, taking a half-hour detour through the overgrown alleyways of Gamsutl, half-buried under the stones of collapsing houses, before we reach the path to Sogratl.

Abduljalil points to a low hill in the middle of the village where human bones spill out of caves whose mouths had been blocked with large rocks. There are shinbones, shoulder blades and jawbones scattered about, and we are told that skulls can also be found. It is the site of a pre-Islamic burial ground where the distant ancestors of Gamasutlans rest. Abduljalil tells us that researchers from Makhachkala once asked to excavate the graves, but were refused permission by the *jamaat*. 'The *jamaat* was right. Why disturb the dead for some stupid research,' says Abduljalil. 'There was one guy who started building a house in the village. He needed some clay to reinforce the roof, so he dug up the graves along with the bones. He didn't wake up the next day. A storm came in, bringing hail, and the roof caved in on him. The dead deserve respect regardless of their religion.'

* * *

The cemetery resembles the more impressive necropolis of Dargavs in Northern Ossetia. Small stone structures, each of which is the tomb of a single family, take up the larger part of a hill overlooking the village below. Each tomb contains human remains that remain very well preserved due to the unique microclimate. Rather than being buried or cremated, the bodies are simply stacked one on top of the other, with the father on top, the grandfather beneath him and then the great-grandfather beneath them. You can touch the yellowed, twisted corpses clad in tattered rags, look into their sunken eye sockets, hold their hands.

Respect for the dead and ancestor veneration only partially explain why these cemeteries have survived untouched for centuries. Why did the imams and priests not order them razed so that people would forget their ancestors who lived in the 'darkness of disbelief', just as the sacred pagan groves were cut down during the Christianisation of Europe? Islam arrived in Daghestan much earlier than Christianity did in Poland, and yet it would be ludicrous to expect any Pole to know which cemetery their pagan ancestors were buried in. Pagan cults, Judaism, Zoroastrianism, Christianity and Islam: these religions appeared in the Caucasus in this chronological order. Yet the rise of each new religion did not bring with it the complete eradication of earlier beliefs. Old religious practices simply made room for the new. In the contemporary Caucasus, Muslim Azeris and Lezgins celebrate Nowruz, the spring festival with roots in Zoroastrianism, while some may practise fire worship. Easter is celebrated by the older generation of Muslim Kists (Georgian Chechens) living in the Pankisi Gorge, while Armenians or Svan people in Georgia sacrifice animals in their holy places in the presence of their priests.

There is no point in saying this tradition is pagan or Christian, or this is not Islamic. Religious practices in the North Caucasus are another example where we cannot speak of 'one true Islam'. It is wiser to ask what it means to be a good Muslim. And this may include celebrating Nowruz.

* * *

Gamsutl slowly disappears from sight, shrouded in thickening fog. We enter the forest. The light drizzle has given way to heavy rain, and it has become unbearably cold. Abduljalil doesn't seem to mind, and stops every hundred metres to go off on philosophical tangents about Sufism, the ethical and moral teachings of the local *adat*s and finally about his own personal idea of combining all the world's major religions, which he claims would bring about peace on earth—all of which we would be thrilled to hear, if it weren't for the icy rain pouring down our collars and the mud sucking our feet in up to our ankles. We get lost in his ramblings after a while, but not wishing to offend our guide and philosopher, we nod or shake our heads depending on his tone of voice, and take turns pretending to follow his thoughts.

Our talkative guide unexpectedly falls silent. Abduljalil rubs his beard, glancing apprehensively at a nearby clump of bushes.

'Hush! The jinn!²'

'What?'

'The jinn!' he repeats a bit louder once the bushes have disappeared around the bend in the path. 'There was a man who didn't believe that there were jinn there. He went and peed in the bushes.'

'What happened?'

'They killed him, that's what happened! They came to his house and strangled him. There's no joking with the jinn!'

3

'WAHHABIS'

We hear the muezzin's call to prayer in the distance. The village is hardly an impressive sight from afar. The capital of Andalal is technically a historic settlement, but most of the homes are new and topped with steep sheet-metal roofs.

The contemporary history of Sogratl has not been spared its share of bloody events. The village's inhabitants have not been particularly fond of either their Soviet or Russian rulers. Nor did they get along with the nearby village of Chokh or other neighbours such as the Laks, an ethnic group once known as the Kazi–Kumukhs, both of whom once pledged their allegiance to the tsar, and later to the Bolsheviks. The people of Sogratl have always gone against the grain, a choice that has often brought suffering upon their village.

Sogratl also played an important role in the Caucasian war against Russian rule. The uprising of 1877 erupted during the final nineteenth-century war between the Russian and Ottoman Empires. An inhabitant of Sogratl, Muhammad-Haji as-Suguri (the son of Abd al-Rahman as-Suguri, one of the closest advisors to Imam Shamil) was chosen as the leader of the uprising. Just as Gunib was Shamil's last line of defence in 1859, so the fall of Sogratl marked the end of the 1877 insurgency. Russian retribution was extraordinarily bloody. As-Suguri was hanged in front of his family, along with over a dozen other leaders of the uprising. Thousands of Daghestanis were deported to Siberia, among them 400 inhabitants of Sogratl. The *aul* itself was burned and razed on orders from the governor general of Daghestan, Armenian Mikhail Loris-Melikov. Sogratl is by no means an *aul* of doctors and professors. One might describe it as a village of *ulamas* and *qadis*, or scholars and Muslim judges, respected not just in Daghestan but throughout the entire Middle East.

Sogratl was home to one of the Caucasus's most famous madrasahs—religious schools attended by future Muslim clerics—prior to the Soviet Union's mass persecution of religion in the twenties and thirties. The village is also the site of the tomb of the Naqshbandi Sheikh Muhammad al-Yaragi, the spiritual leader of the Daghestani uprising against the tsar in the nineteenth century, and the teacher of the imams Ghazi Muhammad, Hamzat Bek and Shamil.

We wander through the winding alleyways of Sogratl. With our feet soaked we make no effort to avoid the muddy streams rushing over the narrow streets. We finally stumble into the courtyard of one of the large, recently renovated houses. 'Ahmed, you've got company!' Abduljalil calls out, visibly excited as he invites us into the home of a surprised middle-aged man. He does not look pleased. It is obvious that our host had been on his way out just a moment ago. 'They've come all the way from Poland,' the beekeeper explains, as if acting as our agent, undeterred by the look on the man's face. The fact remains that we have clearly come at the wrong time. 'Welcome!' sighs Ahmed. 'A guest in the house is God in the house.'

* * *

Shivering and soaking wet, we are long overdue for some tea and a bite to eat.

'Why don't you go wash up first,' Ahmed offers. His suggestion seemed somewhat presumptuous, but with our drenched coats and our trousers caked up to the knees in mud, an opportunity to clean up was more than welcome. We probably should have offered to do so ourselves. In the Daghestani mountains, where bathrooms are far from common, it is considered polite to ask the host for a basin of water in which to wash one's hands or feet before sitting down at the table.

Our host brings us a clean change of clothes. A short three-stripe tracksuit, a close-fitting men's T-shirt, a pink women's top with an image of the Spice Girls and two pairs of new white socks. We are grateful for dry clothes but cannot help but giggle when looking at each other.

Ahmed's bathroom is truly impressive. Such amenities as a bathtub, a shower and hot running water are a truly rare occurrence in the Daghestani countryside. Luxuries such as these can only be afforded by the most resourceful and wealthy villagers. The rest must make do with washbasins in unfinished bathrooms set aside back in the USSR, when the dream of paradise seemed to be just around the corner. The outhouses found in the yards of most homes are neat and clean—even out in the sticks. Every outdoor toilet has a watering can in the corner. Thoughtful hosts will put out some toilet tissue (or strips of newspaper), knowing that 'Russians and the rest' have different customs and may feel confused and will often forget to fill up the watering can beforehand.

* * *

Despite our insistence, Ahmed decides against going out to see his friends. He is helpful and follows the rules of local hospitality, but for some reason he doesn't strike us as particularly trustworthy. He also has a creepy habit of staring. Oblivious to our host's dissatisfaction, Abduljalil continues his philosophical musings, making the atmosphere more and more slumberous. Ahmed has long stopped listening to the monologue. Every now and then he is hurrying his visibly exhausted wife with bringing in the dinner.

Two men suddenly appear at the door. One is tall and stocky. His serious face has a few days of grey stubble. He wears glasses with thick lenses. His companion is short and inconspicuous, wearing a leather jacket and jeans with the legs rolled up above his ankles. Could they be 'Wahhabis'?

'As-Salamu alaykum!'

'Wa alaykum as-salam!' They shake hands only with the men. Women are greeted with a nod of the head.

Their discussion continues in Avar, but we can tell by their gestures that they're talking about us.

'Get ready. We're going on a trip,' says one of them offhandedly. The men seem untrustworthy and weird. The rain is coming down so heavily that we can't see the house next door. We quietly hope that we are in fact going on a trip.

We pile into an old Volga. Abduljalil unexpectedly grows sullen. He gazes pensively at the water streaming down the tinted windows.

'Sogratl is an old historic settlement,' offers the inconspicuous companion, before falling silent once again. Tell us something we don't know. For instance, why are we being driven outside the village? We can't help but recall the story of two Polish researchers, Zofia Fischer-Malanowska and Ewa Marchwińska-Wyrwał from the Polish Academy of Sciences, who were kidnapped not far from here in 1999. The professors were visiting Daghestan on invitation from the Institute of Biology at the Russian Academy of Sciences. They were planning on spending a few days at the research station in Gunib. Instead, they spent a few months in captivity, taken hostage by Chechen militants. We stop in front of a new stone building, from which we have a panoramic view of

Sogratl. The sign on the gate reads 'Watan [homeland] Memorial Complex'. We breathe a sigh of relief. It seems we had fallen victim to the media's stereotypes about 'Wahhabis' supposedly kidnapping people on every corner.

The Watan Memorial Complex, which we end up visiting, contains a stone tower, a mosque, a small museum and a cobblestone courtyard. It was built to commemorate the victory of the Daghestanis over the better-armed, more numerous and better-trained army of the Persian Shah Nadir, who invaded Daghestan in 1741. Nearly all of Daghestan's nationalities and independent mountain communities joined forces in the culminating battle that took place in one of gorges near Sogratl. The complex commemorating the event was built a few years ago with funds from one of Sogratl's most wealthy inhabitants, Gamzat Gamzatov, president of the Dagenergo electric utility company. Both Gamzatov and the Watan memorial are the pride of all of Sogratl. 'If only we had known what the Russians would end up doing to us, we wouldn't have fought off the Persians,' comments the inconspicuous one. 'Who knows? Maybe we'd be better off now.'

His views may be described as very bold. In Daghestan, few people oppose the republic's allegiance to the Russian Federation. Even fewer admit to such opinions openly. The dominant view in public discourse is the one expressed by Daghestani poet Rasul Gamzatov, who once said that 'Daghestan did not enter Russia willingly and neither will it willingly secede.' There isn't even a hint of irony in that statement. While Daghestanis can hardly be described as submissive, separatist movements have gained little ground. Although we might think of the Caucasus as a 'freedom-loving' region that yearns to break free of Russian 'imperialism', our view of the Northern Caucasus is largely affected by Chechnya, which happens to be the exception rather than the rule. Daghestanis are more pragmatic than their neighbours to the west. They realise that without their right to work in Moscow and without federal subsidies from Russia, the republic would not survive for long. No one knows what might happen if Moscow ever fails to pay up.

* * *

The downpour resumes and we take cover in the Volga. The 'Wahhabis' are once again driving us somewhere. Peering through the fogged-up windows, we see little more than brush and a mountain river gushing through the valley below. We finally reach a metal gate. Behind it stands a large, unfinished house, a few rows of beehives and a sizable orchard. 'This is my fazenda,' Ahmed says, making no attempt to mask how proud he is of his wealth (the world of Brazilian soap-operas has managed to infiltrate Daghestani speec. patterns: dachas are for the poor; the rich build fazendas or haciendas). We realise what we're in for. What else besides drinking can one do on a rainy afternoon at a dacha (or rather, fazenda)?

The 'Wahhabis', both about fifty years old, turn out to be very devout Sogratlans permanently residing in Makhachkala. They become more talkative after a while, but not under the influence of alcohol—Ahmed doesn't even offer them any. It seems they just trust us. Their laconic remarks soon give way to a sad tale about people who are not permitted to live differently from others. Differently, meaning in accordance with their own consciences; in keeping with their strict, self-imposed rules.

'It's gotten to the point where people are afraid to let their beards grow. They were constantly being harassed by the police,' the one in the glasses complains. 'I've been stopped in Makhachkala five times. Each time they took me down the police station and questioned me. I got so sick of it that I ended up shaving it off. If you go to the mosque regularly—especially the main mosque—you're immediately suspect. God forbid you pray differently from others. Wahhabi!'

'Even the people praying next to you could be snitches. If you show up too often, they'll start keeping an eye on you.'

'Raids happen almost every day. They check your house for religious books and alcohol. I keep a half-empty bottle of vodka in my fridge, just in case.'

Beatings, kidnappings, torture, the planting of drugs and weapons, forced confessions and threats against family members are all common occurrences. In many cases, alleged 'Wahhabis' taken into custody wind up dead. Police reports later claim that the suspect died after jumping out of a window during questioning. What these reports fail to mention is that police department windows are equipped with thick metal bars. Men who sport beards or lead 'overly devout' religious lives aren't the only ones who run into trouble. Russian converts to Islam, of whom there are a growing number in Daghestan, also face persecution. Even a woman wearing the hijab can find herself under attack. 'Whoever heard of a Daghestani woman, a highlander, wearing "Arab" clothing?! A miniskirt, high heels and a half-inch layer of lipstick—why not? But the hijab? She must be a Wahhabi! A terrorist! An enemy of the nation!'

'All we're trying to do is to be good Muslims.'

'Have you performed the Hajj?'

'No, they won't let us. You have to receive permission from the Spiritual Board of Muslims of Daghestan. And like everyone in Daghestan, the Board

ɔ the bone. They make fortunes off of the Hajj. In order to
.ave to give them a bribe, and that's against our rules. Maybe
ュ find a way to go.'

* * *

Wahhabis: what does the word actually mean, and who are the people that the Russian government has been using as a sort of bogeyman since the early years of the Putin presidency? Wahhabism can be regarded as a reform movement in Islam referring to Muhammad ibn Abd Al-Wahhab teachings. It emerged within Salafism, a broader reformist movement. Al-Wahhab, similar to other Salafis, called for a return to 'pure' Islam, decrying the 'sinful' polytheism and departures from the faith of Muhammad that he saw all around. He preached that earthly power could only belong to Allah, who in the Qur'an and the Sunnah gave mankind instructions regarding not just morality, but also socio-political systems, the economy and all other areas of life. Al-Wahhab forbade the worship of saints and graves, the use of talismans and prayer beads and friendship with followers of other religions. He considered all those who did not adhere to his teaching to be heretics. His principles lay at the foundation of the national ideology of Saudi Arabia and inspired the formation of similar movements in other parts of the world.

But what does this have to do with the post-Soviet Caucasus? Who are these local 'Wahhabis'? Fundamentalists? Terrorists? Fanatics? All of these are buzzwords that provoke more questions than they offer explanations.

A dictionary entitled *Islam in the Former Russian Empire*, published in 2006 by the Russian Academy of Sciences, describes 'Wahhabis' or 'Salafis' as adherents of a radical, reformed Islam which appeared in the former USSR in the late nineties. They are all Sunni Muslims—like Abd al-Wahhab—whose goal it is to 'hand over to Allah the rule of lands inhabited by Muslims'; in other words: to create Islamic states in these lands and to replace secular order with Sharia law.

But what does this have to do with our two 'Wahhabis'? Most likely nothing at all. The point is that just about any 'overly devout' Muslim in Daghestan can find himself called a 'Wahhabi', a label which has become nothing more than an invective.

This is especially true of independent-minded Muslims who profess their own views and criticise the secular and religious powers. If you wear a beard, you're a 'Wahhabi'. If you don't drink or go out for girls, you're a 'Wahhabi'. If you perform the *salah* five times per day, if you don't steal public property, you're a potential terrorist. But why? This attitude certainly isn't fuelled by an overzealous approach to national security. For just a few dollars, anyone can transport a bomb, a Kalashnikov assault rifle or even a Kamaz truck full of armed militants across one of the many police checkpoints in Daghestan. The government requires an internal enemy it is able to portray as a threat, not just to the citizens of Daghestan but to the central government in Moscow. An enemy who will serve as a scapegoat for every crime and every murder that is in fact a result of the struggle for power. An enemy that can be used to fight all independent-minded citizens, all those whose existence inconveniences the government in any way, such as journalists or human rights activists. Political opponents may simply be denounced as 'Wahhabis' or their clandestine sympathisers. The number of captured 'Wahhabis' affects a politician's ability to earn promotions, secure funding for 'the war on terror' and gain power.

* * *

The secular government isn't the only power responsible for the ongoing war against 'Wahhabism', which began in the late nineties. The campaign was also initiated by the official Muslim clergy and the leaders of Sufi brotherhoods, known as sheikhs or *ustaz*. The imams and mullahs belonging to the Spiritual Board of the Muslims of Daghestan, along with the sheikhs, saw the new groups and branches of Islam that had appeared after the fall of the Soviet Union (including 'real Salafis') as a deadly threat to their own social standing, as well as to their income.

The Spiritual Board is the successor of the official Islamic structures of the USSR. These institutions, which were infiltrated and completely controlled by the KGB, professed a strict separation of religion and state, a concept which they had borrowed from the structure of the Orthodox Church.

Every independent Islamic organisation attempting to preach its own views publicly was stepping on the toes of the Board, especially if it voiced its disapproval of the imams and sheikhs through sermons, books and newspapers, accusing them of violating the principle of *tawhid* (strict monotheism) by attributing to themselves the powers of Allah (such as the ability to perform miracles). Such organisations would challenge the Administration by openly stating that, according to the rules of Islam, there can be no intermediary between man and Allah; or by accusing the hitherto respected, grey-bearded, *papakhi*[1]-wearing imams of knowing less about the Qur'an, Sunnah and Sharia law than they did about folk traditions and local witchcraft; or by condemning them for not knowing their own religion and keeping the people in the dark. Such radical, unambiguous views found fertile ground in many social circles, particularly among young people.

Finding themselves in dire straits, the official clergy and their Sufi allies launched a counterattack, taking every opportunity to denounce 'Wahhabis' (i.e. religious activists expressing views different from theirs) as terrorists and foreign intelligence agents. They accused them of attempting to tear Daghestan away from Russia and introduce Sharia law, plunging the republic into the darkness of the Middle Ages. They even coined the term 'traditional Islam' ('traditional' meaning 'Daghestani'), the definition of which was limited to Sufism. Followers of all other branches of the Muslim faith were to be regarded as heretics. The Sufi–Salafi dispute that erupted in Daghestan in the nineties would surely have been limited to theological debates, were it not for the alliance between the Spiritual Board and the politicians in charge of the republic. Not only did the former feel threatened by the rise of independent Islamic organisations but they also needed religious legitimisation for their political administration, which was structured upon clan and mafia-based ties. The government would receive the clergy's blessing, recognition and assistance in controlling society, and in exchange it would offer its help in fighting 'the Wahhabi heretics'; a classic marriage of the altar and the throne (although the latter does not exist in Islam). The witch hunt had begun. It continues to this day as cruel and ruthless as the fight for power and wealth. The worst part is that society initially approved of the campaign, having been conditioned by years of propaganda to accept simple answers to complex problems—answers that made it clear who was good and who was evil, who was the enemy and who was a spy, a terrorist and a fifth column.

* * *

It is time for the evening *salah*. Our 'Wahhabis' ask for a basin of water and a towel. They go into the next room to pray. Ahmed pours a shot of vodka. 'You want to see how our "Wahhabis" pray? You can go snap a picture,' he mumbles, half drunk.

4

MAALI

It was around six in the morning. A group of passengers had gathered in the centre of Sogratl to wait for the *marshrutka* to Makhachkala. When the van pulled up, it was almost full. Some of the more resourceful Sogratlans had already reserved a spot with the driver. A few purse-wielding women managed to secure the rest of the seats.

'These are my guests from Poland,' our host intercedes. 'You can't just leave them behind.'

A solution was found: the local boys piled on to each other's laps and some-one pulled out the ubiquitous wooden stool and placed it in the middle of the aisle, freeing up three seats (Abduljalil decided to accompany us). We feel sorry for the poor passengers who had no choice but to give up their seats. Perhaps instead of going back to the city we could somehow make our way into the neighbouring district? We have been told that a Christian Orthodox church, or what's left of it, survives to this day in the village of Datuna. Bidding farewell to Abduljalil, we get off at the Gunib GES,[1] a new hydroelectric power plant recently built on the river Kara Koysu, supplying energy to the entire valley. The driver refuses to take the bus fare from us. 'You're guests!'

We climb toward the pass dividing the Gunibsky and Shamilsky Districts. The gravel mountain road, which appears on the map to be a more heavily travelled and even sealed route, is completely deserted. There is nothing but rocks and silence. The roads connecting Makhachkala to the *raycenters*[2] are usually of decent quality, but the same cannot be said of the roads between them, particularly ones that run through isolated mountain valleys. There's

25

usually no transportation, there might be but a path worn by sheep browsing for food. On rare occasions when locals visit neighbouring districts they instinctively switch to Russian, the only language in which they can hope to communicate away from home. And they put the seat belts on—the patrolmen are no longer 'theirs'.

Approaching the pass we see a gravestone made out of sandstone. We stop for a while. It must have been a respectable person: a sheikh or *alim*. Or a beloved family member who died in a car accident. A branch stuck into the rocks hardly copes with the many headscarves tied to it. In front of the gravestone there is a Sprite can with some plants in. Gravestones of sheikhs or *alims* turned into pilgrimage sites (*ziyarat*s) are abundant in Daghestan: at the cemeteries, near springs, waterfalls or hidden deep in the mountains. Passers-by stop, pray or think of a wish, tie a scrap of cloth on to a nearby tree or branch, or leave a few rolled-up roubles for good luck. If they commute, they slow down and lower the volume of the music.

* * *

Leaving the pass far behind, we reach a narrow river running along the bottom of a deep canyon. 'Maali' reads a freshly cut wooden sign on a bridge decorated with green flags. Could it be some Muslim holiday? We haven't had a bite to eat since this morning and, even worse, we've run out of water. The walls of the canyon are too steep to risk a trip down to the stream. But how could we possibly miss such an event? According to the map, Maali is still 10 kilometres away uphill.

'Let's go'—we decide.

'Maybe someone will give us a lift.'

The occasional car passes by on the dusty road. We stick our thumbs out once, twice, three times. Nothing. That's odd. Hitching a ride seldom takes more than twenty minutes in Daghestan. Maybe it's because of my outfit. Trousers, a T-shirt and no headscarf. Is Maali a 'Wahhabi' village? I duck behind a knoll to change into a skirt and tights and cover my head. Still nothing. Worse still, the traffic is growing lighter with every passing minute.

The surrounding mountains appear rugged and menacing, and the landscape is becoming increasingly moon-like. All around us are grey, dry rocks. How could anyone settle in a spot like this, with so many beautiful locations to choose from in Daghestan? Some stunted apricot trees grow on an isolated flat patch of earth. Where do they get water? How do locals water their crops and orchards on the mountainsides? Not that we're concerned about the irrigation system used in the Gergebilsky District (Maali, as we later learn, lies in this administrative district). We're just thirsty. We walk 3 metres then take a break. Three more meters and one more break. We continue in this manner for an hour, like pilgrims or penitents. We flag down a car approaching from the opposite direction to ask for a sip of water. We must have truly been a sight for sore eyes: before we can say a word, the driver pulls out from under his seat a half-full bottle of Deneb (a pear-flavoured soft drink) and a bag of sweets. Thankful to the driver, we can move on. There are more and more cars coming down the hill. Is the celebration over?

* * *

We manage to catch a ride with two boys in a Lada, who drive us up the last 2 kilometres of the road. Our arrival causes quite a stir among the villagers of Maali. The eyes of several hundred villagers are fixed on us. Changing clothes did little to help, despite my best intentions. My thin headscarf and calf-length skirt are about as modest as a bathing suit compared to the golden-brown, baggy coats and hair-tight scarves preferred by local women. I'm beginning to think we've ended up in a 'Wahhabi' village. The locals' velvety dresses and long headscarves are all too similar to the ones I once saw in Gubden. The village appears rather wealthy, with large, freshly renovated houses. Just like the ones in Gubden.

* * *

Gubden, February 2006

'No pictures!' yell the chador-clad women of Gubden, glaring menacingly at us from behind their black veils. Some angrily cover their faces with their scarves, though they appear curious of us.

'Why did you come here? A woman wearing trousers? And with no headscarf? We have different rules here, you know! Get out of here!'

We put our cameras away and head over to the local market to find some appropriate head coverings.

'These are very expensive,' the saleswomen announce, somewhat presumptuously. 'And old.' Time has certainly taken its toll on the scarves, leaving holes and bare patches. But to demand a half thousand dollars for a golden-brown piece of cotton sold out of a cardboard box spread out on the ground? Who buys these things? As it turns out, the inhabitants of Gubden are traders and antique collectors. Their vast, palace-sized homes often hold impressive collections of furniture, fabrics and antique china, which the villagers buy in

Moscow and Bronisze, near Warsaw. The 100-year-old golden-brown scarves are their most prized items.

More and more women appear at the bazaar dressed in niqabs. How is that possible? Such an outfit would be grounds for arrest in Makhachkala, or would at best prompt a search of the woman's apartment and a background check on her husband. Men don't seem to hide their Salafi views here. They are sporting full beards, shaved moustaches and rolled-up trousers; their faces appear calm and deep in thought.

Gubden is one of the so-called wealthy Salafi *jamaats*. Their inhabitants, who are traditionally very religious, have adapted to the reality of the market economy and haven't the slightest intention of sharing their profits with the corrupt authorities. Nor have they felt the need to submit to any religious supervision. They don't want their children drinking away the family fortune in 'video arcades', saunas and dance clubs like their urban peers. Life in the village is regulated by Sharia law. Secular courts have been replaced by their Sharia counterparts, while the local administration serves a merely symbolic function. In practice, the laws of the Russian Federation do not apply in Gubden.

The police have been forced to adapt to the local order. Any attempts to enforce their mandate would end in decapitation, or at best a quick change of address. Policemen thus cover for locals and, at their request, keep tabs on strangers. Having received complaints from the women at the bazaar, the police spring into action. The officers take us in for questioning and, after asking us to cover up, take us on a tour of the village in a squad car. In the evening we are dropped off at one of the antique and hi-fi equipment-filled mansions.

Like in many parts of Chechnya, local law enforcement officers in Gubden must have been 'retrained' to serve as morality police. The kind that enforces the ban on the sale of alcohol, which isn't even served at weddings (at least not openly), and makes sure that women conduct themselves appropriately. They also chase away any 'decadent' strangers that dare sneak into the village with cameras, which remind the villagers of the methods used by the security services. While the FSB has thus far turned a blind eye to the rule of Islamic law in the village, they may receive orders to subdue this 'terrorist enclave' at any moment. There are over a dozen such communities in Daghestan, although no one knows their precise number or location. They don't announce their views or call for jihad. They're simply there. Have we wound up in one of them?

* * *

After a while, a young man finally approaches us and strikes up a conversation. Others join him, and the tension subsides somewhat. Apprehensively, we pull out our cameras and start taking pictures. Despite our fears, the villagers approve.

We were lucky to have arrived just in time. Refreshments are served on rugs spread out on the school soccer field. Our appearance in Maali has raised a serious dilemma for the locals. At such ceremonies in Daghestan, men and women are required to eat separately. Or, more precisely, the women eat after the men have finished. It would be inappropriate to seat a woman with the men, especially one with braids poking out from under a flimsy headscarf. The opposite arrangement is equally unthinkable. After a prolonged, feverish debate, they come up with a solution: we are to be seated together in the kitchen, away from everyone else.

We find out that today was the official opening of a newly built mosque. Imams and sheikhs from all over Daghestan have gathered for the events, as have Maali natives scattered throughout the country and the former USSR.

After dinner, a young boy named Ahmed, who has likely been appointed to 'take care' of us, offers to show us the new mosque. The impressive building is made of polished beige rock (the most common construction material in Daghestan) and features a green dome, a soaring, unfinished minaret and new plastic windows.

'As non-Muslims, you can't go inside. I tried to talk to the elders, but they wouldn't change their minds,' he says shyly. 'But you can look in through the door.'

Perhaps it's a question of my inappropriate headscarf and immodest dress. But it is extremely rare for a man not to be allowed into a mosque in Daghestan. In many other Daghestani villages we were permitted to visit mosques. I was usually just asked to cover my head, and even that rule was sometimes waived. When I see the green twig pinned on the door of the mosque, I begin to wonder whether the presence of an infidel at the opening of a mosque is believed to bring bad luck.

'That's to protect it from spells,' Ahmed explains without a hint of irony.

The new mosque can easily hold between 200 and 300 people. The interior is spacious and empty. It is clean and neat, though modest: so different from the old mosques, which are decorated with colourful, often floral, motifs. The floor is covered in blue-grey wall-to-wall carpeting instead of rugs. Scattered here and there are *tubeteikas*, a kind of skullcap worn by Muslims, particularly Turkic ethnic groups. The inauguration prayers must have just recently ended.

Inside there is a centrally located *mihrab* (semicircular niche), indicating the direction of Mecca, and next to it are engraved passages from the Qur'an. There are neither wallpaper-sized photographs of Mecca nor tapestries depicting Imam Shamil, which are popular in many village mosques in Daghestan. 'Upstairs there is a separate room for women'—explains Ahmed. Men are not supposed to see women while praying, but women rooms usually offer a view of the men below. At the entrance there is a space resembling a washroom, in which Muslims perform their ablution before the *salah*, washing their feet, hands and faces.

* * *

The women, wrapped in scarves and cloaks, and the mean-looking bearded grandfathers in *papakhi* hats gladly posed for pictures. The teenagers snap photos of us using their latest model cellphones, straight from Moscow electronics stores.

'Are you going to publish pictures of our holiday in the paper?'

'No, online.'

'What's the address?'

'www.kaukaz.net'

A teenager named Maga connects to the Internet on his phone and quickly pulls up the page. The boys browse through our photos of the Caucasus with interest. Older villagers gather around them, commenting on the site.

'Are you going to write a post about our village? Hold on, I'll take a picture of you too. We'll post it on our own website.'

We didn't know anything about Maali and its inhabitants before we arrived. There are no attractions in the Western sense of the word. No traveller known to us has ever passed through here, and if any have, none have written about it. No counterterrorist operations or hunts for 'Wahhabis' have ever taken place here. Simply put, nothing has ever happened here that would attract attention from journalists or travellers. And yet Maali is one of the most dynamic, optimistic and open Daghestani villages we have ever visited.

* * *

Telmen, the local schoolteacher, invites us to stay the night. We learn from him that Maali is a very religious village. Many Maalians have performed the Hajj. Every woman in the village wears a headscarf, even the youngest ones. Very little drinking goes on in the village. 'I don't generally drink but we will have just one little glass each of my homemade cherry liquor [*nastoika*]. I keep it for special occasions'—says Telmen while pouring a red liquor into our glasses during the supper.

Telmen tells us about the history of the *aul*. The inhabitants of Maali are Avars, but they consider themselves Maalians above all else. Their identity is strongly tied to the *jamaat*. They speak their own dialect, which is only about 30 per cent intelligible to other Avars. To preserve their traditions and language, the villagers practise arranged marriages, almost all of which take place within Maali.

The village was once home to Georgians, who arrived in the tenth or eleventh century for reasons that remain unclear. They might have been seeking shelter from the conflicts waged between Georgian dukes, or simply moved in hope of a better life. They may also have been Georgian missionaries, many of whom travelled to Daghestan in that period, achieving great success in propagating the Christian faith among the pagan Avars. We know that local Georgians left the region around the fourteenth century, which supports the missionary theory. Harassed by the raiding armies of Tamerlane, Georgia could no longer afford to support missions north of the Main Caucasian Ridge. All that is left of them is a cemetery, the ruins of a village consisting of about 150 houses and a handful of place names referring to Queen Tamara that point to a historical Georgian presence.

Christianity in Daghestan has a long tradition. It was practised until the seventh century by most of the inhabitants of southern Daghestan, which, along with the northern part of what is now Azerbaijan, belonged to Caucasian Albania at the time. The faith had been brought to the region by Armenians in the fourth century. Western Daghestan, meanwhile, remained under the influence of Georgian Orthodox Christianity from the tenth to the fourteenth century. Arab raids in the latter half of the seventh century sparked the gradual but consistent Islamisation of Daghestan, which soon became the main Muslim centre of the Caucasus. It wasn't until the Russian conquest of the region that Christianity once again appeared on Daghestani soil.

Georgians in Daghestan aren't just the descendants of settlers or missionaries from the south. Daghestani highlanders, known for their raids and prowess in battle, often ventured into the lands of their southern neighbours to kidnap men and, more often, women, whom they would hold for ransom or keep as slaves. The descendants of these slaves eventually earned their freedom, but feeling more Daghestani than Georgian, they remained in their adopted country, giving rise to separate clans with recognisably Georgian surnames. While Daghestanis eventually came to recognise them as their own, the two groups very rarely intermarried. For a person from a respected Daghestani family to marry someone of Georgian lineage would have been considered a *mésalliance*. Does this hold true nowadays?

'It doesn't matter as much as it used to. Georgian, Daghestani: what's the difference?' a young girl explains.

'And is there anyone of Georgian descent in your family?'

'Of course not! We're *uzdens*.[3] We have nothing but blue blood in our veins!'

* * *

Maali differs from most other Daghestani *aul*s in that its inhabitants don't grumble about the economy, low wages, unemployment and corruption; nor do they complain about their misfortune or the government. Could they really be so hopelessly optimistic? Or is their bread simply buttered on the other side? The latter appears more likely. The official Maali website (www. maali2005.narod.ru) features a list titled 'People we're proud of', containing the names of deputies, judges, businessmen, a policeman and an employee of the Ministry of Internal Affairs. All of them support their community financially or have used their connections for the benefit of the village. One of the donors provided a transformer in a time of need and secured a 50 per cent discount for villagers on the Maali–Makhachkala *marshrutka*. Another donor contributed to the mosque construction fund. Connections are just as important as the thickness of one's wallet. The community values those who can pull its members up and help them find jobs. It is not uncommon for certain positions or branches of industry to be 'occupied' by people from a single region or even village. This appears to be a contemporary dimension to a longstanding Daghestani tradition, according to which each village has its own specialisation. For centuries, the *aul* of Kubachi has specialised in manufacturing silver products. The inhabitants of Andi are famous for their burkas and felt, while Balkhar is known for its pottery. Meanwhile, the village of Chokh, which we visited earlier, is an *aul* of professors. Khosrekh and Tsovkra are home to famous composers and circus performers, respectively. Kumukh, locals claim, has given Daghestan its finest cosmonauts (one so far, but another one is already in training). And Maali? Discussions with Maalians reveal that the *aul* is known for its police officers. It is true that quite a number of the village's young men have found jobs with OMON, the Special Purpose Police Units used wherever regular law enforcement fails. They are sent to subdue Salafi villages, disperse protests and maintain order at mass events. OMON may not be highly regarded in the Caucasus, but it does help with *razborki*, or conflicts between neighbouring villages, and can prove invaluable when a girl's parents won't give her hand to her kidnapper, making it necessary to recapture the maiden.

Telmen fondly recalls an event that took place the previous year. A certain young *dzhigit*[4] from the next village kidnapped a local girl without her consent. The girl's parents were adamantly opposed to the wedding. Maali's OMON servicemen wasted no time in getting their colleagues together, while relatives and neighbours pulled their AK-47s out from under their beds. They snooped around the area and talked to the right people, and soon surrounded the house in which the girl was being kept. The romantic *dzhigit* escaped through a window and ran for the hills.

'It is not a secret that almost everybody's got a gun here'—says Telmen. 'I have no idea about machine guns [*pulemyot*] but half of the armoury could most probably be found here'—he laughs, 'That's how we live. You never know what happens.'

* * *

We didn't reach the Orthodox church in Datuna we were heading for. It turned out to be less than 20 kilometres from Maali, but we made it there only a couple of months later. Unintentionally.

Two guys from the *raycentr* of Urada wanted to have a beer with us and at the same time not be seen in the village. They offered to take us to the local tower in the nearby gorge, where local youth come to have fun.

We followed the tiny path along the river in the gorge. After a twenty minute walk, we took a turn right and what we saw was not a tower ... but Datuna church! The two guys wouldn't believe it was not a fortress or an old mosque. Datuna church is situated on a big rock and surrounded by streams from three sides. The church's 1-metre thick walls are largely intact but decorated in contemporary 'aphorisms' spray-painted in Avar. Broken beer bottles and watermelon rinds left by picnicking youths litter the floor.

This tiny medieval Georgian church is one of the best-preserved traces of the republic's ancient Christian history. The church was built at the end of the tenth century and was the longest-used Christian house of worship in Daghestan. It was abandoned in the thirteenth century with the spread of Islam, only to be used again in the eighteenth century long after Islam had taken over in these parts.

It was in 1849 when a group of Old Believers[5] persecuted by the Russian government fled to the North Caucasus and asked Imam Shamil to let them live on his land in an isolated place. Initially, they built their villages on the forest hills of Dargo-Vedeno in Chechnya, but some of them eventually resettled in the Khatan–Bugob–Kkal[6] gorge near Datuna church, which they used as a house of worship. Their community existed until 1852.

5

THE JINN

In the name of Allah, the Entirely Merciful, the Especially Merciful. Say, 'I seek refuge in the Lord of mankind, The Sovereign of mankind. The God of mankind, from the evil of the retreating whisperer—who whispers [evil] into the breasts of mankind—from among the jinn and mankind.'

Qur'an, Sura 114 (an-Nās)

There was an old inscription in Arabic on the heavy, wooden door of his house. He led us there without so much as asking us who we were and what we were doing there. There was an extraordinary sense of calm about him; he virtually glowed with inner peace. He wore a black and white *tubeteika* on his head, a threadbare grey sports coat, and ancient, tattered shoes. His lean face was covered in stubble. His black eyes were somewhat sunken, his gaze piercing, yet at once absent, as if he were staring off into the distance.

He lived in the small *aul* of Koroda. It is one of those places where something peculiar—an elusive aura—hangs in the air. The village, the canyon leading up to it and the surrounding mountains are simply there. They exist. They've stood there, immobile and utterly silent, for time immemorial, shrouded in mystery. Enormous black boulders, vultures perched on the rocks, apricot trees—and people. Taciturn and quiet, as if absent.

He approached us as we were standing in front of the mosque, from which he had just emerged with a group of young men, most likely friends of his. They had just finished noon prayers.

'Come to my house. We'll have some tea and talk. It would be a great pleasure to have you in my home. My name is Musa.'

Topped with a soaring minaret, the mosque stood atop a hill overlooking the new village of Koroda, linked by a natural stone bridge to the old *aul*, which was slowly dying out and crumbling into a heap of rubble. The houses in both parts of the village were built so tightly that the streets between them formed an irregular labyrinth, one cut off from the rest of the world by steep cliffs. We followed Musa into the maze of nooks, stairways and streets. Inaccessible to cars, Koroda is only navigable on foot or by donkey, plenty of which could be seen wandering the village.

Musa stops frequently to point out and translate the Arabic writing adorning the walls and doorways of houses along the way. He falls silent and says a short prayer as we pass the cemetery. Musa appears very devout. Could he be a mullah? At such a young age? But then again, why not? Where would middle-aged mullahs have been recruited? There weren't many clerics in Soviet times. Official clergymen usually collaborated with the authorities and enjoyed little respect.

* * *

This was the first place in which we were not offered alcohol. The fact that it was the middle of the day was hardly the only reason. Instead, we were given Kalmyk chai, which resembles Mongolian milk tea. It is a slightly sweet but greasy brew with a skin floating on the surface, and is said to be healthy and nutritious. Luckily, it was spring, and not yet the season for *kurduk*—a kind of mutton fat rendered from the animal's fleshy tail. While it is certainly a question of taste, it is truly hard to take a liking to these two elements of Daghestani cuisine. Musa's wife, a modest woman in her twenties, served us *plov*, also known as pilaf—a rice dish cooked with carrots, garlic and either mutton or beef. She would not sit with us.

* * *

Bismillah—'In the name of Allah,' our host prays before sitting down to eat. He makes the symbolic gesture of washing his face. Musa's young daughter waited on us while her mother peeked out from behind the door.

Musa was no mullah. He supported his wife and children by running a small shop in nearby Gunib. He was also a self-taught artist—a sculptor and painter. He found inspiration in Islam, of which he was a devout follower, and in the good jinn. He spoke of them with great awe, telling us how impressed he had been with a video he had recently watched depicting the jinn in action.

At first, we thought he was speaking of yet another revelation depicted in movie film from the cellphone photo galleries we were shown beforehand: the famous lion in Baku whose roar was said to sound like the word "'Allah',." a crow or bull praising God, a sheep whose coloration formed the Shahada, the Islamic creed, or shots of the 2004 tsunami in South East Asia depicting waves that supposedly spelled out "'Allah'."

But Musa's knowledge of jinns was impressive and by no means superficial like ours. Having barely heard of jinns in Islam, we still remembered more about jinns in Sindbad and the *Arabian Nights*.

Jinns—which should not be confused with angels or demons—are mentioned in several parts of the Qur'an. 'And I did not create the jinn and mankind except to worship Me,' says Allah in the fifty-first sura, Adh-Dhāriyāt. The jinn were born of fire. They inhabit deserts, crevices, mountain passes, rubbish dumps, cemeteries and other out of the way places. The word *jinn* comes from an Arabic root that means 'to be hidden'. Jinns cannot be seen, although they do, on occasion, assume the shape of (usually naked) humans, snakes, dogs and other animals. They have the power to move around quickly. Just like humans, jinn exist in both male and female form. And just like humans, they belong to families and nations. There are Muslim and non-Muslim jinn. Some are good, others are evil; some are benevolent, others are mischievous. Every person has his own jinn. It coaxes people into doing evil deeds. The presence of jinn in our world is manifested through apparitions, visions of the future, prophecies and dreams. According to Islamic tradition, jinn eavesdrop on angels and pass this knowledge on to people of their choosing. But the angels guard their secrets jealously, and throw fireballs at the jinn to drive them away—hence the existence of meteors and falling stars.

Evil jinn occasionally enter and possess humans, taking control of their bodies and minds. The victim of such a possession can only be saved through exorcism. Following the example of the Prophet Muhammad, any 'true' Muslim can evict evil jinn by reciting the appropriate verses from the Qur'an. Most people, of course, seek the assistance of imams, sheikhs and other respected figures—Muslim exorcists who aren't afraid to confront evil forces.

Musa shows us videos of one such séance on his mobile phone. The exorcist talks to the evil spirit, coaxing it into accepting Islam or repeating verses from the Qur'an that praise Allah. The jinn is cajoled, but not coerced. The cleric speaks in a calm yet firm and powerful voice, asking the spirit to leave the person's body, which is sometimes racked with such convulsions that several strong men are needed to restrain it. The jinn hisses, wheezes, roars, spits and curses, resisting expulsion. In the end, it subsides and relents. It leaves, relieving the possessed.

* * *

Musa calls his daughter and shows us her amulet inscribed with Qur'anic verses which offer protection from jinn. Such amulets are given to children and adults, and hang in cars and homes to protect from the evil jinns. (Some, especially the more reformist-minded, claim that these practices are antithetical to Islam, just like horoscopes, fortune-telling and other practices considered 'witchcraft'.)

The formula *Bismillah*—'In the name of Allah'—is intended to ward away evil spirits and avoid offending the vengeful jinn. Musa says it should be uttered before entering a home or bathroom, before eating, opening a hot water tap or disrobing (people are more vulnerable to jinn when naked)— before 'opening' or 'beginning' anything, in general. It is also forbidden to relieve oneself into holes in the ground, which may be inhabited by an innocent jinn who could be deeply offended by the act. Increased vigilance is also recommended at night. The howling of a dog or the braying of a donkey after dark is a sign that the animal has seen a jinn or the devil. When saying (or reading) the *salah*, one must be careful to make sure a donkey, black dog or even a woman does not cross in front of him.

* * *

Musa's involvement with the jinn was no coincidence. In pre-Islamic times, Arabs believed that every artist had a personal jinn who watched over his talent. Perhaps our host was an exorcist as well. Perhaps he could talk to the jinn. Did they listen to him?

6

JIHAD

'We're waiting for an answer from the tunnel,' explains our driver—an unshaven man dressed in stained sweatpants and a worn-out leather jacket—when, after two hours of waiting, we impatiently ask if we would be moving on soon.

Every once in a while, a bored passenger pounds the radio with his fist. Not out of anger: an hour or two makes little difference in these parts. The radio simply won't play without a firm hit. At the nearby bus stop, *marshrutka*s bursting with passengers depart for Khasavyurt and Grozny, just a few hours' drive from Makhachkala. Trade and shipping are booming between the Daghestani capital and North Ossetia and the Kabardino–Balkar Republic. The drivers can't complain of a lack of passengers.

'*Shayze kullare*(Why won't you look at me) ...?' Lively Avarian music plays over the stereo: an indispensable element of every *marshrutka* in Daghestan.

The road into the mountains leads through a tunnel near the village of Gimry. The tunnel has been closed off as a result of a KTO[1] (pronounced as separate letters, *keh-teh-oh*)—a several-month-long counterterrorist operation. The region is officially closed to traffic, and drivers must make a detour of almost 100 kilometres. *V printsipye*, or *technically*, the tunnel cannot be crossed. But the stress is always placed on that magical phrase, *v printsipye*, which embodies the local attitude towards rules of all sorts. 'You can do anything, as long as you do it carefully.' Our driver finally decides to go for it. We head off, stopping by the 'Gimry' gambling parlour in the town of Buynaksk, where our driver drops in to consult with what must be a credible source: who is on duty today, will he let us through and, if so, for how much?

We try to glean some information from the other passengers: 'What's going on over there?'

'Nothing much. A special operation. But it's really just money laundering.'

'What?'

'They've kept an entire army in the village for half a year just to capture a few "Wahhabis"', the driver chimes in, spitting sunflower seed shells on to the floor. 'They love doing that around here. There were still burned-out tanks lying in the ditch south of Buynaksk not too long ago. In the end, people just took them apart for scrap metal.' 'Not too long ago' was 1999. The outbreak of full-scale war was quite possible at that time. Busy with its own affairs, Moscow exerted merely symbolic power over the region. The de facto independent Chechnya, governed by the militants who emerged victorious in the 1994–6 war, threatened to deepen the instability in the entire Caucasus. Heavily armed and led by former field commanders, criminal gangs based out of Grozny, Gudermes and Urus-Martan did as they pleased in Chechnya and neighbouring republics. Human trafficking surged, while kidnappings for ransom committed by Chechens became such a common occurrence that people were afraid to leave their homes after dark.

The late nineties were also a high point for the activity of Daghestani Islamic radicals, led by Bagauddin Kebedov (popularly known as Bagauddin Muhammad), now in hiding somewhere in the Middle East. This uncompromising follower of 'pure' Islam organised an illegal religious group as early as the 1970s, before moving on to political and propaganda activity after the fall of the USSR. Like the seventeenth-, eighteenth- and nineteenth-century Muslim theologians and thinkers such as al-Yamani, ibn Taymiyyah, al-Wahhabi and al-Kuduki, now regarded as the ideologists of Salafism, Bagauddin called for Muslims to return to strict monotheism (*tawhid*) and—most importantly—to establish the 'rule of Allah' wherever they lived. Applied to the realities of Daghestan, this could only mean the replacement of the secular political system with one ruled by Sharia law. As the government in Moscow was highly unlikely to have accepted such a solution, it became necessary to 'liberate' Daghestan from Russian rule. Bagauddin's followers, like other, less radical opposition Islamist activists, took full advantage of the chaos reigning in the Caucasus at the time and the relative freedom they enjoyed in Russia under Yeltsin. They preached their beliefs openly and held debates with members of the official clergy and Sufi sheikhs. They had their own mosques, madrasahs, publishing houses, and controlled a few settlements. Bagauddin's radical views led him to forge an alliance with Chechen militants, most notably Shamil Basayev. Although the ideology of most Chechen politicians of the time was rooted in nationalism, Bagauddin resolved to make an alliance with them and use their well-armed and trained troops to further his own goals in Daghestan. After a failed attack on a Russian military base in Buynaksk in December 1997, Bagauddin's forces made a retreat to Chechnya. Described as a 'minor Hijra', their escape was likened to Muhammad's flight from Mecca to Medina. In Chechnya, Bagauddin's followers preached the 'liberation' of the entire Caucasus from the rule of the kafir (infidels), convincing Basayev and Khattab, the Saudi-born leader of the foreign mujahideen, that the inhabitants of Daghestan were just waiting for the signal to launch an insurrection against the government. Locked in conflict with Chechen President Aslan Maskhadov and thirsty for glory, Basayev was easily swayed.

In August 1999, Bagauddin led Daghestani mujahideen from Chechnya into the Tsumadinsky District, where they seized several villages. They proclaimed the Islamic Republic of Daghestan and called for a nationwide insurrection. Basayev's forces came to their assistance a few days later in the neighbouring Botlikhsky District. The mujahideen soon attempted to take Khasavyurt—the second biggest town in Daghestan. To Bagauddin's surprise, the insurrection failed to materialise, a turn of events that infuriated Basayev. What's more, the attack ended in a humiliating defeat.

In the eyes of the Daghestanis, Bagauddin had committed unforgivable treason by seeking help from Chechen forces. The locals responded by pulling their AK-47s out from under their beds and setting off into the mountains of Daghestan alongside the Russian army, with whom they defeated the invaders in a matter of days.

Heady with its victory over Bagauddin and Basayev's troops, the Russian government decided to rid itself of yet another problem: the 'Wahhabi' enclave in the Buynaksky District, which our driver referred to when he mentioned the burned-out tanks in the ditch.

Consisting of a handful of Dargin villages, the enclave was an area in which local Islamic radicals implemented the concept of the Islamic state in 1998–9. Irritated by the inertia of the republic's administration and the lawlessness of the Daghestani police, the group decided to take matters into their own hands. The armed men chased the government and police out of their villages and proclaimed their land a 'free Islamic territory'. They formed their own army and set up checkpoints on local roads, collecting a toll from passing vehicles. They imposed Sharia law and set up Islamic courts. A radical-controlled *shura* (council) took over the so-called *Islamic Djamaat of Daghestan* and appointed a Sharia police force, which punished theft by cutting off hands and meted out beatings with truncheons for such transgressions as alcohol consumption or women uncovering their heads. Was this barbarism? From our point of view: yes. But they saw it as an escape from the corrupt, oppressive and incapable Russian state.

Thus was formed a deadly alternative to the regime in Makhachkala, which tolerated the *Jamaat* only out of fear of sparking an internal military conflict. In the summer of 1999, when the tug-of-war between radicals and federally backed Makhachkala came to a head, the Daghestani regime decided to do away with the Kadar 'Wahhabis' once and for all. At its request, Russian soldiers encircled the entire *Jamaat*. They did not even offer to let them surrender their weapons. They simply started firing. No one was expecting any white flags, anyway. The siege lasted about a week. The villages of Karamakhi and Chabanmakhi were completely destroyed, along with the militants defending them and the inhabitants who had failed to flee in time.

The idea of an Islamic rebellion in Daghestan had fizzled out. Bagauddin and his people's sole 'achievement' (and the sole 'achievement' of Basayev, who had let himself be talked into the whole mess) was that they had given Moscow a pretext to send their military into Chechnya, starting the second Chechen War and ending the republic's three-year period of quasi-independence. Bagauddin fled to the Middle East, while a cruel wave of repression targeted at so-called 'Wahhabis' (real and imaginary) swept across Daghestan. A bill on the fight against 'extremism and Wahhabism' was rushed through the Daghestani parliament to provide legal grounds for the operation. The events appeared to spell the end for Islamic radicals in Daghestan, who would nevertheless return to make headlines again just a few years later.

* * *

Outside of Buynaksk, the *marshrutka* begins a steady uphill climb. The surface of the road grows worse with each hairpin turn. We're surrounded by nothing but forests covered in fresh May foliage. The villages have disappeared; gone are the ubiquitous cows napping in the middle of the road or sauntering majestically along the shoulder. The music is turned down and the talking is cut short. The tunnel draws nearer. From afar, we can see an armoured personnel carrier parked across the road. There are clouds of smoke everywhere.

Equipped with a bulletproof vest, an AK-47 and a few grenades tucked into his belt, a fair-haired sergeant with a broad, Slavic face unenthusiastically scans the passengers, likely cursing the day he was taken from his hometown of

Voronezh or Kursk to this 'wild' land to hunt for 'Wahhabis' among a strange people, purportedly for the greater glory of the fatherland.

'Vasya dear, come with us. We'll find you a fiancée and throw you a wedding,' the woman sitting next to us tries to joke, with badly feigned honesty. But there's no need for it: Vasya isn't too involved in his duties, anyway.

'That's enough now. Give me your passports. I need the men to step out for registration.'

'The soldiers are rather polite,' we try to strike up a conversation with the talkative passenger in her fifties, who, as we learn later, turns out to be the wife of a former KGB officer.

'They make money off of it: they have to be polite. They take 500 roubles per car. It's highway robbery! Besides, they're afraid of our guys. They're scared stiff, so they keep their mouths shut.'

'They're afraid of our guys ...' Do any of the Russian soldiers based in the Caucasus share this belief? They seem more like ruthless mercenaries that destroy entire Chechen villages, murder civilians and rape women. But many of these boys brought in from somewhere in the Ural Mountains or Kaliningrad are simply frightened. They're afraid of the strange world that surrounds them and the strange people who smile at them, pat them on the back and pour them shots of vodka, only to shoot them from around a corner a moment later, slash them across the ribs with a knife or tip off their pals lurking in the forest. These boys want to go home to their mothers and girlfriends. They couldn't care less about the whole Caucasus, this whole mess in Chechnya and Daghestan. Nor do they care about Putin and his struggle for the 'territorial integrity' of Russia. Is this supposed to be Russia? The Crimea, Odessa, Minsk—sure. But Makhachkala? Grozny? Vladikavkaz? They kill or drink the fear away. They drown it in drugs or mindless cruelty that they later regret and which comes back to haunt them in nightmares. Or they just keep to themselves and avoid sticking their necks out. They pretend to serve. They pretend to check *marshrutka*s. They pretend not to see the rifles sticking out of the trunk, the trigger marks on index fingers, the hateful stares and the ostentatious spitting.

* * *

The smoke-enshrouded, gaping darkness of the entrance to the tunnel resembles a gateway to another world. The soldiers huddle in front of a fire for warmth, roasting potatoes over the flames. The ground is littered with tin cans and empty moonshine bottles. We move on. Our driver switches on the windshield wipers. The several-kilometre long tunnel looks as if it has just been carved into the rock. It is dark inside; water drips from the ceiling, and the road alternates between bone-shaking bumps and a muddy sludge that sucks the van in over its tyres. The mountain seems ready to collapse, burying the tunnel along with anyone who dared venture into it. A tiny light greets us in the distance after we round the last of many bends.

We drive into the counterterrorist operation zone. We see military towns capable of housing thousands of soldiers; tanks, armed personnel carriers, military patrols and field kitchens. Down in the valley, nestled among rocky, fantastically shaped ochre outcroppings, a village drowns in blooming apricot orchards. Its inhabitants, outnumbered two to one by the soldiers, have been accused of practising 'Wahhabism' and lending support to Islamic militants.

* * *

Gimry. The gate to the mountains. It is said that every trader once had his own *kunak*, or friend, in the village, with whom he could stay before heading off into the mountains. Gimry was the home *aul* to two of the three nineteenth-century Chechen and Daghestani imams: Ghazi Muhammad, whom the Russians refer to as Qazi-Mulla, and Shamil. Two figures who led the highlanders on a jihad against the Russians and their local, feudal supporters. It was here that years of unrest were thought to have finally been suppressed in 1832. After a few days of fierce resistance, the *aul*—in which nearly all of the insurgents led by Ghazi Muhammad had taken refuge—was taken by the Russians. A few, among them Shamil, managed to escape the siege and the subsequent massacre carried out by General Rosen's troops. Legend has it that the body of Ghazi Muhammad, who refused to abandon his men, was found in a praying position, confirming the belief that *shahid* (martyr) militants go straight to heaven for their faith. His body was taken to the village of Tarki at the Caspian Sea, where it was buried. It was feared that the grave would become a destination for pilgrimages by the local highlanders. Shamil, however, ordered a secret exhumation of the remains, which were finally reburied at the Gimry cemetery.

How wrong the Russian strategists were to report back to St. Petersburg that the rebellion had been suppressed. How they regretted having let the yet-unknown Shamil escape encirclement. He would go on to wage jihad for twenty-five more years.

Who is fighting in Gimry today, and what are they fighting for? The offensive is officially being described as a counterterrorism operation, a hunt for 'Islamic terrorists'. But it is hard to believe that this is the real reason an army of several thousand troops has been kept in a single village for half a year. Forced to pay more for *marshrutka* rides, the locals see the operation as a plot by the military to make a profit off travellers and the inhabitants of the village. Others suspect that the presence of troops is somehow tied to an army-run money laundering scheme and some conflict over budget funds set aside for the construction of a hydroelectric power plant on the nearby river and for the repair of the Gimry tunnel.

Islamic militants may indeed be present in Gimry. But the same can be said of tens of other Daghestani villages. The Daghestani-born professor, Enver Kisriyev, who studies these issues in Moscow, claims that the republican government is behind the operation. By pacifying the rebellious village of Gimry as a supposed refuge for 'Wahhabis', Daghestani former President Mukhu Aliyev wanted to set an example for others and show them that the government would not take the rebellion lying down. The reason he chose this particular *aul* was that it is inhabited by Avars, a nation to which the former president himself belongs. Mukhu thus aimed to demonstrate that he treated all citizens equally, regardless of nationality, and that contrary to earlier accusations, there would be no favouritism or leniency for the Avars.

No Daghestani politician, however, is stupid enough to pick a fight with any local community. Especially with the inhabitants of Gimry, who are famous for their fierceness and tenacity. Had Aliyev sent the Daghestani police or any other local force to the village, the participants of the operation would have been held personally responsible for any blood spilled or insults committed during the pacification of the village. In Daghestan, there is no such thing as collective responsibility for harm or murder. 'Even if an entire crowd were to trample a person, the one who actually did it would be held responsible,' explains Kisriyev. And thus the spiral of violence is drawn tighter by the tradition of vendetta: Caucasian highlanders are required to avenge the murder of a relative or—just as importantly—a mere insult. The former president thus persuaded the Kremlin to send the army to the village. Gimry's 'Wahhabis' would be unlikely to track down Sergeant Ivanov in Pskov or Private Popov in Chelyabinsk to avenge the death of a son or the beating of a father. And even if they did, it wouldn't have been Mukhu's concern.

* * *

Jihad. The so-called 'holy war'. It has been going on in Daghestan for several years. On one side is the entire state apparatus with the police, military, prosecutor, courts, prisons and tanks. On the other, a group of young people, likely numbering a few hundred, hiding in forests, the homes of relatives, neighbours, friends and sympathisers. Hunted, tracked and murdered, they fight back fiercely, ruthlessly executing members of the security forces and Muslim clerics collaborating with the government. Not a week goes by without a shooting, a bombing or an assassination. The authorities conduct one special operation after another, cordoning off entire villages or boroughs and sending in tanks, armoured personnel carriers and helicopters. They take no prisoners. They used to, but juries would sometimes acquit the insurgents, infuriating the military. Despite continuous losses, jihadi forces keep returning, to attack again the very next day.

They do not fear death; they seek it. They look at pictures and watch videos on dozens of illegal Islamic websites, dreaming of one day dying the death of a *shahid*, crying 'Allahu akbar!' They have become idols to a growing number of young Daghestanis. What are these teenage boys and girls fighting for? In the name of what have they resolved to give up their lives? The goal of modern-day Daghestani militants, regardless of their allegiance (to the Caucasian Emirate or the Islamic State), is nothing less than to 'establish the rule of Allah on earth'. Yasin Rasulov, a young journalist and scholar, and one of the ideologists behind the Daghestani militant movement, wrote in his doctoral dissertation (which he defended before joining the jihad) that 'modern-day militants have not invented anything new'. According to him they are merely continuing the work of previous generations. Ghazi Muhammad, Hamzat Bek and Shamil all fought for the same goal, as did the insurgents of 1877. The rebellions sparked by Najmuddin Gotsinsky and Uzun Haji following the Bolshevik Revolution shared that goal as well.

But what exactly is 'the rule of Allah', a concept that seems unfathomable to many of us?

What it means is the establishment of Sharia law, which is based on the Qur'an and the teaching of Muhammad (the Sunnah). It is a law that encompasses and regulates (at times in great detail) every area of life, from issues regarding religious worship, through the relationship between a husband and wife, to the political system of the state. People—who are described in the history of Islam as the 'Servants of Allah' and live only to praise him—are expected to submit to this law completely and unquestioningly.

According to some readings of the Qur'an and Sunnah, an orthodox Muslim should not live under the rule of kafir, who prevent him from living according to Sharia law, in turn keeping him from salvation. He cannot abide by their laws. If they rule over Dar-al-Islam (the land of Islam), he must either undertake a hijra—move to a country where Sharia law is respected—or start a jihad (holy war) in order to liberate himself from the rule of non-Muslims. That—nothing more, nothing less—is the direct statement and goal of Daghestani militants.

Are they madmen? Are they blind radicals? Are they chasing utopia? The Bolsheviks, with their fight to topple the tsar, abolish private property and establish the 'dictatorship of the proletariat' while throwing bombs at tsarist officials, also struck others as crazy, and their ideology was considered madness. Yet they ultimately seized power and managed to impose their insane ideology on society.

It would be a mistake, however, to attribute the jihad to a band of renegades and religious fanatics. In the militants' ranks, simple country boys fight alongside doctors, former entrepreneurs and even people with PhDs. Their choice to join the jihad is not driven by poverty or—as government-paid journalists claim—because they receive a stack of dollars for every police officer they kill. They grew out their beards and picked up rifles because they could not find a place for themselves in a country where nothing counts as much as connections and money. Where one cannot get an education or a job without bribes and contacts. And—most importantly—where people cannot practise their own faith and abide by its rules. No drinking, no smoking, no whoring, no stealing, no cheating. Many of them were 'helped along' in their decisions by the security apparatus. It is not uncommon for a militant to have gone through the hell of Daghestani jails before heading out into the forest. Jails in which, to this day, methods are used that resemble those described in Solzhenitsyn's *Gulag Archipelago*:[2] denailing, electric shocks, police-baton rape, mock executions and unambiguous references to the detainee's wife and children.

The rule of Allah, which the Caucasian militants are now fighting to establish, has more than just a metaphysical dimension. Their struggle has an entire practical goal as well: to achieve social justice. Many of those fighting for this idea aren't war-hardened 'professional terrorists' trained by Bin Laden's men in the deserts of Afghanistan, but boys and girls who couldn't find a place for themselves in the world they lived in. They are non-conformists who care enough to fight. Assuming this perspective, a 'terrorist', 'Islamist' or 'religious fanatic' may suddenly become a person who has made a dramatic choice. An idealist prepared to die for an idea. Perhaps we may then come to the conclusion that we must find other methods of dealing with Islamic terrorism than the war on terror. The problem is that policy-makers in Washington, London and Moscow don't have time to think. They need quick and simple solutions like the ones provided by their terrorism experts. For the latter, such doubts are little more than red herrings, a waste of time and a display of weakness. And so the jihad continues ...

7

SHAMIL'S SIBERIA

It was growing dark. The torrential rain and rocks falling from the stone cliff above didn't seem to bother the two young *dzhigits* appointed by the FSB officer in Agvali to escort us to the village of Tindi. As they tore down the road at a frightening speed with the stereo blaring Russian *popsa* music, we couldn't help but remember the news that was on everyone's lips in the mountain districts: a *marshrutka* had recently fallen into a river in the Tsuntinsky District, killing eight passengers. We would hear it from everyone wherever we went, but the event seemed to have no effect on Daghestani drivers, judging by the speeds at which they drove along the mountain roads.

The gorge was growing narrower. We had left behind the Andi Koisu river, which carves through the highest mountains in Daghestan, and the village of Agvali—the 'capital' of the Tsumadinsky District, where we spent a few memorable moments with the heads of the local police, municipality and FSB.

Allahu akbar! Allahu Akbar! The muezzin's call briefly interrupts our interrogation.

'There's something suspicious about you.' The officer stared at us silently. Was he hoping we would break down under his piercing gaze and admit to being American spies?

'Why do you say that?'

'Does a normal person have this many stamps in his passport? What am I supposed to do with you? Look, this is a border zone. Georgia is just over the mountains, and we all know what that Saakashvili's been up to. And tomorrow's the inauguration of President Put ... I mean Medvedev. You realise what this looks like, don't you? They're holding the presidential inauguration in Moscow, and we've got foreigners snooping around down here.'

'But we're just—'

'You sit here for a minute. It's time for noon prayers. I'm going to pray and then we'll decide what to do with you,' he says, pulling out from under his desk a small rug depicting the Holy Mosque in Mecca. On returning (from what we later discovered was a small prayer room), he consulted with FSB chief Ahmed. The latter turned out to be more good-hearted and laid-back than we had thought, and he kindly gave us permission to remain in his district. But he never let us out of his sight as we walked around Agvali searching for transportation into the mountains. 'Why ask for trouble? This is a border zone.'

* * *

The Tsumadinsky District is in fact situated on the Russian–Georgian border. It is also close to Chechnya, which lies just across the Snegovoi (Snowy) Ridge. The district became one of the most 'remote' areas of Daghestan and among the most forsaken corners of the entire Caucasus. It is connected to the rest of the republic by a single road that winds along the cliffs overlooking the Andi Koisu river. The trip from Makhachkala to Agvali takes a whole seven hours, very long by Daghestani standards. Reaching the remaining villages in the district is even harder. Not all of them are connected by sealed roads. There are still *auls*, such as Khushet near the Georgian border, that can only be reached on horseback or on foot. To buy groceries in Agvali, the villagers of Khushet must walk over 30 kilometres along a narrow path worn by their ancestors.

No one ever succeeded in permanently subjugating Tsumada. The impenetrable mountains, the snow-clogged passes, the deep, dark gorges and the almost complete lack of roads served as an effective deterrent to would-be invaders. But with the region's sparse arable land surrounded by rock, cliffs and glaciers, there was very little reason to conquer it in the first place. The Tsumadans of centuries past made a living by planting crops on terraces, raising sheep and cattle and marauding in nearby Georgia, where they would rob caravans and raid the courts of Georgian dukes, taking prisoners for ransom and even marriage. It is said that to this day, 'scary Daghestanis' serve as a kind of bogeyman used by Georgian parents to scare their children into obedience. Interestingly, Tsumadans themselves enjoy telling the same anecdote, barely containing their pride.

Not only did the inhabitants of Tsumada succeed in fending off external threats but, they also resented their own masters and never allowed an aristocratic class to emerge in their communities. Individual Tsumadan villages—Khushtada, Tlondoda, Echeda, Kvanada, Tindi, Gakvari, and others—were independent city-states of free highlanders, not unlike the ancient Greek *polis*, and banded together into confederations when under attack. Each village was ruled by its own *jamaat*, or council of elders. It was they who decided when to go to war, when to make peace, and when to enter into alliances with other villages. The only authority beside the *jamaat* were the Muslim clerics, but even the imams and the ulama regarded the word of the *jamaat* as sacred.

Thanks to the long-lasting isolation and tiny size of the local communities, Tsumada has witnessed the survival of several ancient—and mostly unwritten—Caucasian languages and small nations that make up the region's uniquely rich ethnic mosaic. Practically every canyon, and in some places even every *aul* is inhabited by separate ethnic groups speaking mutually unintelligible languages: Bagulals, Khvarshis, Chamalals, Didos and the Tindi, whom we try to reach. They communicate with each other in Avar or Russian. Many *aksakal*s (elders) also speak Chechen as in the past Tsumadans would travel to the much richer and fertile Chechnya in search of work.

* * *

Despite the unfavourable conditions, we finally arrive in Tindi. Our hosts—the principal of the local school and his friend, the physics teacher, both designated by the FSB in Agvali—are already waiting for us. In the Caucasus, hospitality isn't just a duty: it is also a break from the monotony of everyday life and a chance to escape the confines of a tiny world. We are thus welcomed without any additional questions such as 'who are you?', 'why are you here?' and 'how long will you be staying?' It is said that guests in the mountains of Daghestan are not even asked their names nor the purpose of their visit for three days after their arrival. Daghestani police seem to be unfamiliar with this *adat*.

'So what'll it be? A little cognac, wine, vodka? I don't drink myself, ever since I swore before the *jamaat* that I wouldn't do it anymore, but Sagid here does. Make yourselves at home. I'll just do my *salah* and we can get started.'

Sagid, who is already preparing dinner at a lightning pace, doesn't need to be asked twice. The glasses are served and the vodka warms our insides. For snacks we have a few Tindi specialties: dried sheep cheese, mutton sausage, honeycombs and scrambled eggs with the famous Tindi onions.

'Go ahead and drink. Don't worry about anything. Leave the *shtraf* up to me. If anyone finds out, that is.'

'The what?'

'The *shtraf*. The 500-rouble fine for drinking. It's the law here. The imam and the *jamaat* decided to ban the sale and consumption of alcohol because it's against Sharia law. Our imam is strict. Even the mayor himself can't get away with a drink. And there's no lack of snitches. We're Muslims, of course, but you can't just completely give up drinking. Sometimes guests show up, or a delegation from Agvali will come to visit, or a Tsumadan wrestler will win a medal. So we drink and we pay up. But it's good that there are these rules.'

As it turns out, the ban on drinking isn't the only Sharia law on the books in Tindi. Also banned are festive weddings, for which the *shtraf* is much higher—15,000 roubles. Often the fine will be paid before the wedding band even arrives in the village. Similar laws apply in most Tsumadan villages. As we were told by a local doctor with whom we shared a *marshrutka* ride, in Khushtada, for instance, women are strictly required to wear headscarves or pay a fine. One exception is Agvali, where one may consume beer freely and attend concerts by Avar pop stars with fancy dresses, makeup and hairdos.

* * *

Are Tsumadans simply more religious than Daghestanis in other parts of the republic? The inhabitants of the most far-flung corners of Daghestan didn't accept Islam until about the sixteenth century—relatively late; the faith reached the southern part of the republic as early as the seventh century. Shut off in their remote gorges, the highlanders practised their ancient pagan beliefs for hundreds of years, combining them with Christian elements borrowed from Georgia. Tsumadans didn't truly accept Islam until the times of Imam Shamil—the nineteenth-century leader of the anti-Russian uprising who imposed Sharia law by fire and sword, burning disobedient *auls* and slaughtering villagers. Shamil must have placed exceptional trust in Tsumadans, as he chose this region—specifically the Tindi Gorge—in which to imprison his enemies. Tindal, or the land of the Tindi, was henceforth known as 'Shamil's Siberia'.

Islam has since become a very important part of Tsumadan social life, and the role of Muslim clerics has increased enormously. The period of tsarist rule did little to change this. Russian authority over the mountains existed only on paper; the highlanders followed their own rules, namely Sharia law and the *adats*. Nor did religious practices die out in this part of the Caucasus in Soviet times. Despite persecution, the murdering of the ulama and the closing of mosques and houses of prayer, children continued to study Arabic, boys were still circumcised, elders abstained from alcohol and women observed the Islamic way of dress. Even the staunchest party activists are said to have slipped out of work on Fridays to fulfil their religious duties in mosques or unofficial houses of prayer.

Perestroika brought about a rebirth, or perhaps greater exposure, of religious practices. But this 'return to tradition' does not yet explain everything. The turn toward Islam and the religion's subsequent assumption of the central role in social life was the highlanders' response to the chaos that enveloped Daghestan after the collapse of the Soviet Union. The meltdown of communist ideology, the collapse of the economy, the disjoint between the government and society, incessant clashes between clans, ethnic conflicts, the war in neighbouring Chechnya: all of this made Islam—a faith that offered its followers a straightforward answer to the question of how to live—the only understandable and acceptable paradigm. The people thus handed real power over to the imams, and agreed to the imposition of elements of Sharia law. Even if they disobey the rules, they appreciate their existence. 'For the sake of young people', 'for the sake of discipline'.

* * *

By morning the wind had swept away the clouds and the fog began to lift from the gorge, revealing the surrounding mountaintops, still snow-capped in mid-May.

'See those women? They're going to work in the fields,' the principal points out. 'Our fields are so steep that no tractor could plough them. There are only two machines in the entire district. Some land is even too hard for the oxen! We send women to tend those fields. They grab a plough and turn the fields themselves!', says the principal with a wink.

'Women, you say. But there don't seem to be very many of them in the village.'

'That's true. They went to work in the onion fields of the Rostov Oblast.[1] They'll be back sometime in the autumn.'

It turns out that onions are Tindi's main cash crop. Most of this farming, however, doesn't take place on the local terrace fields. Instead, nearly all the young villagers—many women among them—set out in spring for leased farm plots in the Rostov Oblast. With only children, the elderly, teachers and the imam left, the *aul* becomes deserted and remains so until late autumn when the villagers come home after the harvest. It is then that weddings are held, and neighbours and relatives are visited. Most locals could move down to the plains where they would lead an easier life. They could settle in Makhachkala or farther away. But there's something that keeps them in the mountains, driving them to come back every year.

There is something uncanny about the connection that Caucasian highlanders have with their native soil. Even when they are forced to leave their place of birth, they maintain their bond with the village for the rest of their lives. They visit the graves of their ancestors, bury their beloved ones at local cemeteries, tend to homes that have long stood empty, teach their children about their roots and try to marry their daughters to men from the family *aul*.

When, in 1957, Chechens returned to their homes after thirteen years of exile in Kazakhstan, they dug up the bodies of their dead and illegally brought them back to be buried in the cemeteries of their ancestors. Even today, with tens of thousands of Chechen emigrants living in Europe, there are only a handful of Chechen graves there. Chechens spend small fortunes to ship bodies back to their homeland and to pay the bribes for the Russian police. The thought of burying their dead in a 'foreign land' is unbearable to them.

For people in the Caucasus, their ancestors' settlements seem to be more than mere places. Even if never visited, their mere existence embodies traditions, *adat*s, language, memories of ancestors that make up a sense of belonging to a particular community, a local identity.

* * *

By now, news of our arrival has spread throughout the *aul*. A 'delegation' awaits us in front of the village administration office: Tindi's only policeman and the chief administrator. We are taken on a tour of the sights, wading through the muddy and littered alleyways of the *aul*. The administrator's shined shoes quickly lose their polish.

We arrive at the *godekan*, the central location of every Daghestani village. The square is a gathering place—exclusively for men. Not to introduce ourselves and exchange a few words would be seen as uncouth. These *papakhi*-wearing grandfathers in shiny-seated trousers have the greatest say in these parts. They were behind the ban on alcohol and festive weddings, and at one time even considered banning tobacco. Anyone who commits a misdemeanour or otherwise misbehaves must appear before the *jamaat*. The old men also serve as peacemakers and mediators between warring families. No important decision regarding the *aul* can be made without their knowledge.

'As-Salamu alaykum!'

'Wa alaykum as-salam! Where are you from?' asks one of the men.

'From Poland.'

'*Polsha?* Tsk, tsk!'

'What do you mean?'

'So now you want a missile defence shield? You're in NATO now.'

'Well, we—'

'You used to be Russian allies. We used to be in the Warsaw Pact together. And now look what you've done. You've sold out to the Americans. What do you think's going to come of that? I'll tell you what: no good. There's no messing around with Russia.'

'But—'

'Oh, we've heard it all. You don't respect veterans. You don't celebrate Victory Day. You've even banned *Four Tank-Men and a Dog.*[2] Isn't that true, Omar? Why don't you tell them; you know all about these things. Omar served Hungary in '56. He helped quash the imperialist uprising.'

'Yeah, but they wouldn't let our brigade shoot, then'—recalls Omar not without a regret. 'We would only go on tanks.'

'If there is anything we could help with while you stay in our village—let us know,' said one of the men when we were about to leave the *godekan*. 'If you want to visit our mosque tell the doorkeeper that I agreed.'

'And thank you for taking interest in our village! *Molodcy*—you were not afraid to come here all the way from Poland! After all this bullshit they say about Daghestan and Chechnya on TV!'

8

SHEIKHS

Murtuz drops us off in front of the home of Sheikh Said Efendi. He won't go in himself, as he doesn't have the highest regard for the sheikh. The house is adorned with green flags; there is a spring and bench for visitors in front. A man with a fierce look in his eyes is explaining something emphatically in what sounds at first to be Avar, but upon closer listening turns out to be broken, guttural Russian. He says that the sheikh is an old, sickly man and is rather busy. He asks guests not to trouble him with prosaic issues such as illnesses, or whom to marry their daughters or sons.

'Only ask religious questions! Do you understand?'

The place appears to be very principled. I realise that I have a bottle of Żubrówka[1] in my backpack. What if they search our bags at the door? Murtuz stealthily finishes his cigarette in the car (we saw no one in the village smoking on the street).

'Here you go! Drink it with your friends!'

'Good luck,' he says, stuffing the bottle into his coat as we get out of the car.

* * *

I'm in real trouble now. I could be accused of sacrilege and thrown out—literally. There's no joking around with Caucasian men. Bowing low, the *murids* run into the carpeted hall and sit down with their legs folded underneath. Everyone is silent: heads bowed, hands on knees. They must be getting ready to pray, I think to myself. What do I do then? They don't look up even when

57

the sheikh comes in after a few minutes. He shakes hands with everyone and begins his collective personal audiences. Where are you from, how many years have you been my *murid*, when did you last see me, what task did I give you last time? The answers are brief and hushed. No superfluous words or unnecessary movement. Complete solemnity and concentration. Some of the *murid*s nervously finger the beads of their *misbaha*s,[2] the 'attribute' of many Sufi. It is finally my turn.

'*Maʿarural*? Are you Avar?'

'I don't speak Avar.'

'What is your *tariqa*[3]?' Said switches to broken Russian.

'I don't have a *tariqa*. I'm from Poland,' I blurt out, shifting uncomfortably as my legs grow numb from sitting on my calves. 'I'm interested in Daghestani Islam.'

The sheikh falls silent. He looks me dead in the eyes with an expressionless stare. The *murid*s glance apprehensively in my direction. The mood has become very tense.

'*Molodets*! You're a good fellow!' A broad smile appears for the first time on Said's grave face. In an instant, the most famous living Islamic leader in Daghestan turned into a kindly, inquisitive grandfather.

'So how are things in Poland? Do you have Muslims there?'

'We do, but not many. Mostly Tatars.'

'I see, I see. And are you a Muslim?'

'No, I'm a Christian.'

'Oh, that's too bad.' Said clicks his tongue and shakes his head. 'You have to take care of that.'

If it weren't for the disarming smile on the face of the old man, who, seeing that my legs were about to give way, gave me a stool to sit on, I would probably be cautious about taking the topic any further. But I decide to risk it.

'I think what's important is that we believe in God. The Qur'an itself says that no one should be converted by force.'

A stunned silence falls over the room. I feel the nervous and impatient stares of the *murid*s. No one else has been given this much attention. The sheikh abruptly rises and, to everyone's surprise, leaves. He reappears after a moment, holding a string of green prayer beads and a book in either hand.

'I like you. Take this and read it. You're always welcome here if you ever want to come back.'

No one says a word over the modest refreshments served in the next room. We eat in silence. It isn't until we go back outside that the *murid*s approach me, shaking my hand and slapping me on the back. We make polite small talk. No one minds that I am not a Muslim.

* * *

The women sit in the back, behind the kneeling men, and whisper to each other. A jittery middle-aged woman elbows me. 'What do I do? Can I look at the sheikh, or am I supposed to close my eyes?'

'I have no idea. I'm not from here—I'm from Poland,' I explain.

'I'm not a local either. I'm from Derbent.[4] People come from all over Russia to see the sheikh.'

I want to explain that I'm not a Muslim, but I'm afraid my outfit is too convincing. My long denim skirt and leather jacket fit the modest female dress code. Even my unskilfully wrapped headscarf, which I constantly fuss with to keep my hair under cover, raises no eyebrows. The women sit in near silence and listen on as the men converse with the sheikh.

'It looks like he's really taken a liking to the tall one! Look how long they've been talking. He must be from far away. *Molodets*!', my talkative neighbour remarks.

'Is he going to come talk to us too, or is it over?' she asks impatiently as the men file out of the room. Said Efendi returns after a moment bearing an armful of prayer beads. He approaches the first woman.

'Why did you come here?' he asks somewhat boorishly.

'I wanted a *wird*, an assignment,' the older woman replies.

'Here.' He hands her a slip of paper with a list of prayers—her assignment for the next few weeks.

'And you?'

'Me? I'm just here to ...' stutters the woman, who has come with her child, clearly confused by the rapid pace of service. She tries to add something, but the sheikh moves on to the next person, with whom he exchanges a few words in Avar and pulls a slip out of a different drawer.

'Did you want a *wird* too?' My turn comes sooner than I had expected. The sheikh offers me a list of prayers. I might have taken this disguise too far.

'No ... I mean, I'm from Poland too.' I can't come up with a more articulate response.

'Poland again? And who was that man to you?'

'A friend.' I immediately sense that the word might sound ambiguous. I should have said 'acquaintance' or perhaps 'brother' or 'cousin'. I feel the sheikh glaring at me.

'We work together. We're conducting research for a university,' I add, attempting to explain that it isn't what it looks like. I'm digging myself in deeper.

'Have a *misbah*.' The sheikh hands me a string of white beads before rising. The women's audience doesn't last long.

As I get up to leave, a minor commotion breaks out. The women run to the sheikh and surround him. They clamour to hand him shopping bags containing meat, tomatoes and sweets. They press 500 rouble bills into his hand, wishing him Allah's blessings.

'It's *sadaqah*'[5]—says one woman.

'We have to wait until the men are done,' an elderly woman explains. After a moment we enter the next room, where a quick meal of pilaf and Kalmyk chai is served. The women dine hastily and graciously pack up the sweets and blocks of halva (made of sunflower seed butter) set out on the table.

'Take it.' A young woman hands me a plastic bag full of sweets.

'It's *sadaqah* from the sheikh.'

Following the women's advice, I also draw sacred water from the spring. 'People come from all over Russia to drink it.'

* * *

This was our first encounter with Daghestani Sufism. Until now we had only read about this mysterious world, which turned out to be surprisingly easy to approach. *Murid, wird, tariqa*: incomprehensible, foreign words. They have been a fact of life in Daghestan ever since the arrival of Islam, of which Sufism has always been an integral part. It is usually described as a mystical dimension of Islam, a tradition whose followers aspire to know God and become one with him here on earth. A person who has achieved this state is known as a sheikh, ulama or *murshid*. In a sense, sheikhs are considered saints within their own lifetimes, as it is believed by Sufis that they can perform miracles, move in time and space, and foresee the future.

One does not simply become a sheikh. A person must be appointed, or to use the Sufi term, be given an *ijazah* from the sheikh under whom he studied as a *murid*. Sufis believe that the *ijazah*s passed on from generation to generation form a holy chain that leads back to the Prophet Muhammad himself. The life of a *murid* is not easy. If the student wishes to be as close to God as his teacher is he must completely submit to him, obeying his every order and completing every *wird*, or assignment. Sufis may experience a taste of oneness with God by performing the *dhikr*, an ecstatic group prayer that sometimes puts participants into a trance.

Early Sufis gathered around charismatic teachers, later forming brother-hoods or orders known as *tariqa*s or *tariqat*s, that is, 'paths', around the ninth century. These hierarchical orders, which exist to this day, have their own practices and follow separate philosophies. While often at odds with so-called 'orthodox' Islam, orders such as Naqshbandi, Qadiri, Shadhili and Suhrawardiyya achieved popularity throughout the Muslim world, from Senegal to India. What is more, Sufism was the reason why many tribes and nations eventually accepted Islam. The fact that Sufism tolerated, and some-times even adapted, pre-Islamic beliefs was a crucial factor. These ancient practices live on in the Caucasus and Central Asia, where sacred trees, moun-tains, rocks and sources are venerated. Where pagan gods were once wor-shiped, there Muslim saints, often Sufis, are now asked for intercession. Orthodox Muslims, particularly Salafis, see this as *shirq* (idolatry), the gravest sin in Islam, while Sufis have nothing against such practices.

Sufism first appeared in Daghestan in the Middle Ages, yet little is known about that period. The recorded history of Sufism in the region begins at the turn of the eighteenth and nineteenth centuries, when Russian soldiers arrived in the Caucasus to conquer the 'inhospitable' mountains for the tsar. Daghestani Sufis, led by the charismatic Muhammad al-Yaragi, initially called only for the observance of religious law. They warned the inhabitants of Daghestan to abandon their sinful ways and to live according to Sharia law. Had the teachings of these 'divine madmen' remained limited to religious issues, the authorities would likely have not even taken notice. But they soon began preaching that all Muslims were equal and that no true-believer should live under the rule of infidels. The reaction of the Daghestani lieges and Russian authorities was not long in coming. They launched a ruthless cam-paign of persecution against the Sufis, who soon joined the insurrection by the Daghestani and Chechen highlanders against the local dukes and Russia, and became their spiritual leaders. This synthesis of Sufism with the anti-colonial and anti-feudal rebel movement led by a series of imams—Ghazi Muhammad, Hamzat Bek and the most famous among them, Shamil—was so powerful that all insurrectionists were eventually labelled *murid*s, and historians named the movement *muridism*. Henceforth regarded as a lethal threat to the empire, Sufis were placed on the Russian blacklist. Overzealous officials were so wary of Sufism that they even persecuted the peaceful Chechen Sheikh Kunta-haji Kishiev, who defied Shamil by calling for Chechens to cease fighting and to lay down their weapons in order to prevent the nation's complete obliteration.

Anti-Sufi policies did not end with the fall of the tsar. Once they had dealt with the Whites and reinforced their power in the Caucasus, the Bolsheviks reneged on the promise given to Muslim leaders to respect Sharia law and commenced a ruthless crackdown. Mosques and Qur'anic schools were shut down or repurposed as museums of atheism; the teaching of Arabic was banned, and Muslim clerics were shot or exiled to Siberia. The NKVD particularly targeted sheikhs and *murids*, subjecting them to the cruellest persecution. The Soviets nevertheless failed in deracinating Daghestani Sufism, which simply went deep underground. But the price it paid for its survival was steep: local Sufism was left degraded—not just as a result of the burning of libraries holding the works of Sufi scholars, the closing of its famous madrasahs and the extermination of its most outstanding sheikhs but also as a result of the complete seventy-year isolation of Daghestani Muslims from the world of Islam, the processes that occurred there and the theological debates that took place in the meantime.

Said Effendi didn't receive any Islamic education. He was a simple country boy who received a revelation while tending sheep in the hills surrounding his family *aul*. Since that time he grew to become the most prominent Daghestani sheikh. He has thousands of murids, many of them influential figures in the government and the Spiritual Board of Daghestani Muslims.

Contemporary Daghestani Sufism is not just about faith and religious practices but also business and politics, as we were soon to discover.

* * *

Sheikh Sirazhuddin Khuriksky's face is oval and rosy, his beady eyes restless. He wears a long cloak and a *tubeteika* on his head. The sheikh confidently marches into the vast carpeted hall in which he holds his daily audiences. He gestures at food spread out on an oilcloth and motions for his assistant to pour the tea.

'You must eat with your right hand!' he barks somehow angrily if not provocatively. He gnaws at a biscuit and washes it down with tea. 'Only the devil eats with his left hand!'

'Fix your scarf! I can see your hair! You're all about alcohol, drugs and promiscuity. Decadent Westerners!'

'Oh you Poles ... You're nothing but trouble. So you wanted to be in NATO, did you? Russia won't let you off the hook that easily, you'll see. Lech Wałęsa? Phooey! Why did he have to go and overthrow communism with American money?'

'But the communists persecuted religion. Islam too.'

'Did they now? Who told you such stories?'

The sheikh seemed to have an answer for everything. We heard from Mikhail Roshchin, a professor from Moscow who visited the sheikh a few years earlier, that he has an authoritative personality. He was forced to perform *salah* with the sheikh. Our visit ended only with a threat of imminent damnation if we did not accept Islam. Sirazhuddin seemed to be busy.

'Get your stuff together,' our host suddenly says. 'I'm heading to Derbent. I can give you a ride.'

The luxury SUV throws up gravel as we tear down the driveway of the sheikh's multi-story house. We pass an enormous gasoline tank in front of which a long line of beat-up Zhigulis wait to fill up. It turns out that Sirazhuddin has monopolised fuel sales in every neighbouring village. His family *aul* of Khurik, which sits among the beautifully forested slopes of the Tabasaransky District, soon disappears behind us in a cloud of dust. Police officers manning a checkpoint along the way greet the sheikh as we drive by. We are in the very heart of Sirazhuddin's territory.

'We're building a restaurant over here, and a hotel up there,' Sirazhuddin tells us, barely containing his pride. 'My *murid*s grow grapes in this village. And we've just finished building a mosque in that one. In Myukhrek we renovated the oldest mosque in all of Russia, and even all of Europe. Nothing goes on anywhere in southern Daghestan without my approval!'

The sheikh-cum-businessman might have been exaggerating, but only a little. He does run a vast commercial empire, and even officials in Makhachkala must take his opinions into consideration. The sheikh answers to no superiors, lay or religious, and cannot be dismissed by anyone. His power is based solely on his religious authority, which in turn relies on the people's belief that Sirazhuddin is bound by an invisible chain to the Prophet Muhammad himself. For those who might have their doubts about this spiritual bond, the sheikh has displayed gold-framed certificates (also available in electronic form) on the walls of his house. According to them, Sirazhuddin received *ijazah*s from Sheikh Abdulla[6] in 1989.

His knack for business and politics is merely an additional attribute, one that Sirajuddin uses with great skill. How can he afford such great investments? Where does he get the money for his mosques, madrasahs and hotels? All of this is made possible by the 'sheikh's noble influence on those who have money,' explains the official website of the organisation Babul Abwab (the Arabic name of Derbent, meaning 'Gate of Gates'), which is headed by Sirazhuddin himself.

The sheikh's *murid*s do in fact include many businessmen and influential politicians, who provide funding and assistance for his ventures. Some do it out of the goodness of their hearts, others do it in order to further the spread of Islam, while others are motivated by their lust for power, which is easier to maintain with the support of an influential religious figure.

The chief administrator of the Tabasaransky District has been trying to ingratiate himself with Sirazhuddin for years. Not that he's a particularly devout Muslim. The sheikh's support simply helps him suppress dissent and gives him an edge over the competition. The chief administrator of the Tabasaransky District paid a hefty sum for the post over a decade ago, and must now regularly pay an *otkat* (kickback) to his superiors, making sure not to be outbid and replaced by a competitor. Some of the cash is said to be pocketed by the president himself. The chief administrator doesn't pay out of pocket, of course. He simply shares with his bosses the money that flows into the regional budget from Makhachkala. Despised by citizens for his skimming and embezzlement, the administrator resorts to any means in order to keep his position. A few years ago, he branded members of the republican anti-corruption committee who attempted to undermine him as terrorists, who can easily be disposed of with the help of security services. To this end, he orchestrated an assassination attempt on himself (sadly, a failed one, his opponents joke). The car (in which he was absent, just in case) 'miraculously' emerged unscathed, but the bomb killed a young girl who happened to be walking by. No one bought the terrorist plot. The poor district administrator must have ended up paying a substantial sum to get the committee members to look for another victim. Investing in the sheikh turned out to be a more effective strategy. Sirazhuddin was pleased with the car given to him as *sadaqah*, and he didn't turn his nose up at a commercial plot, either. In exchange, the cunning district administrator can count on the sheikh's good favour come election day.

* * *

The driver parks in the square in front of the buildings of Babul Abwab. The complex includes a mosque, a madrasah, a university and a newspaper, all of which is under the auspices of Sirazhuddin. All around are the homes of *murid*s, utility buildings, a weaver's workshop and bakeries. Within a moment the sheikh is surrounded by his *murid*s, who bow, kiss his hand and back away without lifting their gazes.

'Maga, come here,' Sirazhuddin calls one of the young men. 'You're going to take them to Makhachkala right now!'

Maga doesn't hesitate for a second. He takes the keys and stumbles into the car. He doesn't look well. It turns out that he has been sick with fever and nausea for three days. He ignores our requests to be dropped off at the bus station. 'The sheikh's word is my command!' he replies flatly as he gets behind the wheel.

It was the obedient *murids* like Maga who in 2005 stormed Derbent's main mosque during noon prayers to deal with followers of a new imam, a rival whom Sirazhuddin had accused of preaching 'Wahhabism'. They tormented the congregation for hours. Knives were drawn and blood was shed. The police did not intervene, and no one was held responsible.

'What happened to the new imam's followers?' we ask Maga, who proudly told us of the events of that day.

'Some went into hiding, others moved to Moscow and some went into the woods and were later caught by special operations forces.'

Sirazhuddin emerged victorious. He could hardly have hoped for a more successful political manoeuvre. Everyone realised that the Tabasaran sheikh was not to be taken lightly, and that he was a clever and bold politician. He would not hesitate to use force to defend his interests, whatever the costs. Though not everyone was pleased with his expanding power, the authorities had no choice but to start taking the opinions of this influential and more respected sheikh into account, and even try to win his favour and blessing. Not only had he become the informal spiritual leader of the republic's entire south but he had also become an important Daghestani politician; a self-righteous, infallible religious leader and at once a successful businessman. A Caucasian counterpart to America's televangelists, but with an army of *murids* in *tubeteikas* instead of white, middle-class families.

* * *

'You visited the sheikhs?!'—asked a reformist-minded friend of mine with a slight distaste in his voice. 'They have nothing to do with Islam'—'I will show you something.' He searches his phone for a YouTube video featuring Sirazhuddin performing *zikhr* with the *murids* in the carpeted room in which we talked to him. 'Look how they are shaking their heads, like at a rock concert!', he laughs.

Sheikhs, both Said Effendi and even more Sirazhuddin, have many opponents, especially among young educated city inhabitants. Why, despite being accused of self-proclamation, of close relationships with the corrupt government and of suspicious business operations, the Sheikhs would still have armies of *murid*s numbering 5 to 10 thousands from Sirazhuddin and twice as much for Said Effendi?

Daghestani Sufism seem to provide people with support, introducing order into the chaotic, 'dirty' world around them, where nothing but money and connections matter. This order was once provided by the state. While it did limit personal liberties and imposed an ideology, it also provided regular salaries and retirement benefits, it offered jobs and promotions and it guaranteed security and stability. The collapse of the Soviet Union was an enormous upheaval that left people to fend for themselves. Warlords, old party bosses and other cunning wheeler-dealers found themselves in their element. Everything was there for the taking. Everyday Daghestanis, meanwhile, have been left feeling helpless and lost. Accustomed to having everything provided and regulated by the state, they failed to find a place for themselves in the new reality of post-Soviet Russia.

It is no wonder that they desperately search for some ersatz replacement of that bygone system, something that would let them feel some form of order in the world: 'one true value' system. They seek someone who, in exchange for their blind obedience, would extend a mantle of security and provide simple answers to difficult questions. Many are amused by the gullibility of the *murid*s. Few stop to consider their needs and the source of their confusion and helplessness. And even fewer offer an alternative.

* * *

Sheikh Sirazhuddin Khuriksky was murdered in October 2011. Two men arrived in front of his home in Khurik. When he stepped out, they fired at him a couple of times before running away.

Sheikh Said Effendi was killed in August 2012 along with six of his followers, including an eleven-year-old boy. A female suicide bomber detonated her explosives in his house which she entered with a group of his worshippers.

9

URAZA BAYRAM

The end of Ramadan, the Islamic month of fasting, is approaching. The markets are filled with housewives stocking up on all sorts of products, from such basic necessities as rice for Uzbek *plov* to crab sticks to put in salads (popular throughout the entire former USSR), to pineapples, a symbol of wealth and luxury without which no table is complete. They buy lemon and orange soft drinks, and even Coca-Cola, which is rarely consumed here, as all heavily processed, Western 'filth' is regarded with disgust. Shoppers scoop up wholesale quantities of chocolate, snack bars and socks.

Unable to find a single open eatery, we purchase boiled corn on the cob from a street vendor. We have barely taken our first bites when a young boy stops to berate us.

'Why aren't you fasting? Shame on you!'

The morality police haven't begun arresting people for breaking the fast in Daghestan, but it is common to be admonished by strangers, particularly neophytes. Somehow we don't feel like eating anymore. We hand our nearly untouched cobs to a Gypsy child who points at them.

In Ramadan, the ninth month of the lunar calendar, Muslims are expected to fast from dawn until dusk. In the early days of Islam, and in the Jewish tradition, the fast only lasted for ten days. It is likely that a conflict with Jews prompted Muhammad to extend the period to one month (he also turned the direction of prayer from Jerusalem to Mecca at the same time). Fasting is a way of purifying oneself of sins; each day's fast begins with the uttering of an intention. During the day it is forbidden not only to eat and drink but even to swallow one's saliva. Other restrictions ban sexual intercourse, the smoking of cigarettes or even the inhalation of tobacco smoke. The period of fasting ends with a holiday that takes different names depending on the tradition: Uraza Bayram (from the Turkish *oruç*—fast, and *bayram*—holiday) or Ramadan Bayram in the Caucasus and Turkey, or Eid-ul-Fitr (Arabic for 'the holiday of breaking the fast') in Arab countries.

* * *

We pack into an overloaded *marshrutka* and head out into the mountains for Uraza Bayram. The bus can barely climb the mountainous road with its steep, hairpin turns.

'That's the Chirkeysk GES.[1] It's beautiful, isn't it?' the woman next to me points out as we drive along the rocky shore of Daghestan's largest artificial lake. One would be justified to assume that it was an enormous landfill that had been flooded, rather than a mountain valley. The azure surface is obscured by a blanket of soda and oil bottles, plastic shopping bags and cardboard.

'It's the second-deepest canyon in the world after the one in Colorado!'

'Too bad it's so polluted,' I remark.

'Polluted? Oh, you mean the rubbish? Yeah ...'

No one apart from us seems to be appalled at the debris littering the lake or the unofficial dumps marring every valley and canyon we pass. That's outside. Most Daghestanis have no qualms about tossing chocolate bar wrappers out the minibus window (but not in Ramadan! God forbid!).They appear not to notice the seas of rubbish strewn about their favourite picnic spots, where they enjoy the landscape and grilled shish kebabs as they stumble over plastic bottles and watermelon rinds. Like 'democracy', the 'environment' is just another word in the Caucasus. Is it a question of habit or upbringing? Or does it come from different perceptions of uncleanliness and order?

* * *

Magomed picks us up in Agvali, the district centre. A friend of ours, his distant cousin, has invited us to Magomed's home.

'Faster, faster,' Aishat urges her husband, who can barely make it around the hairpin turns. We're going deeper into the mountains with Magomed and his wife and son. On left turns we have to keep a cake from flying on to the driver's suit. We begin to get the hang of it after a while.

'The sun sets in fifteen minutes! If we don't make it we'll have to go back!' Aishat sees the surprised looks on our faces. 'That's the custom here. You have to spend the holiday in whatever district you happen to be in when dusk falls. And that's where you give *zakat al-fitr*[2] to the poor.'

'As long as we make it over the pass, we'll be in the next district.' We drive over the ridge just in time, arriving in the village of Kvanada after dusk. The mountain *aul* in the Tsumadinsky District is known for its belligerent stance toward all government institutions. We spend the night in Magomed and Aishat's old, stone house.

'We couldn't see the moon!' Magomed announces, coming home late that night.

'What does that mean?'

'It means we won't have the holiday tomorrow,' explains Aishat. It turns out that the fast cannot be broken until the first sighting of the new moon, which couldn't be seen due to the overcast sky. The imam consequently decided that the holiday wouldn't begin the next day.

* * *

'Our Wahhabis are already celebrating today,' Magomed tells us when he returns from morning prayers. Instead of observing the moon, they simply called Saudi Arabia and synchronised their holiday with them.

'They always have to do things their own way. Lucky for you, actually. You can go eat with the Wahhabis,' Aishat proposes. 'We're still fasting today.' It would be awkward not to feed one's guests, after all. 'Don't worry, they're our Wahhabis. They're good men,' Aishat explains as she gives us directions to the house.

The local Salafis, known throughout Daghestan as 'Wahhabis', are quiet and avoid being photographed. They are safe in Kvanada, where they live in peace with 'traditionalists', who in turn hide them from the police and the FSB, even if the two communities differ in many of their views. To them, every stranger is a potential threat. We often hear about a certain journalist from Makhachkala who wrote in 1999 that there were militants hiding in Kvanada, causing the village to be placed on a list of bombing targets, along with Karamakhi and Chabanmakhi. Local leaders miraculously persuaded the authorities to reconsider their plans. Who knows what we might be planning to write?

Rocks come flying at us on our way back. Some wise-guy also throws a cat in our direction. It might just be a group of kids having fun, or perhaps they're expressing sentiments they picked up from their parents, upset about our presence in the village? If the adults see their brats' behaviour, they do nothing to stop it.

* * *

At dusk, the muezzin calls the villagers to prayer. The *aul*'s narrow streets fill with bearded men wearing leather jackets, sweatpants and sandals. Magomed blends into the crowd of similarly dressed men.

Life in Kvanada is regulated by religious practices. Rarely do people here make plans to meet at a specific hour. They say 'I'll drop by after morning prayers' or 'after the night *salah*'. Even local clocks are set to the prayer cycle. Daylight savings time, seen as inconvenient, has been abandoned, leaving the village in the same time zone as Belarus in the summer, as opposed to the Moscow Time used everywhere else.

Kvanada is the first village in which we did not immediately have to deal with a member of the typical triumvirate: the policeman, the chief administrator or school principal. The most important person in the community is the imam. The local administration has little say in the village. The imam, together with the council of elders, makes the most important decisions, including that of which candidate the village will support in an election. 'Why do people argue over such petty issues? They don't know anything about politics anyway.'

Kvanadans have no need for the state. They do just fine without it. There has never been a police station in the village, even in Stalinist times. Now a beat cop comes by once a month just to check the village off his list of stops. Any problems, including penal offences, are taken care of independently by the *aul*—successfully, in most cases. One example is the conflict between the Salafis and 'traditionalists', which remains a serious issue elsewhere. Few people in Kvanada hold public-sector positions, which are looked down upon (with the exception of schoolteachers). Kvanadans use their own language, Bagvalal, in everyday situations. Many villagers, particularly women, speak little or no Russian. As they explain, they simply don't need it in their "mini-state".

* * *

'Gasan, time for prayers,' Aishat scolds her son.

'Gimme a minute,' he mutters as he sits in front of his computer.

'Not in a minute. To the mosque, right now!'

Muslims are particularly conscientious about their religious practices in the final days of Ramadan, which commemorates the period during which the Qur'an was revealed to Muhammad. It is a time when particular attention is paid to cleanliness. It is recommended that Muslims completely abstain from sexual intercourse, even after dark. Men attend night prayers and hear additional sermons. Meanwhile, Aishat begins her own ablutions before praying (in the Caucasus women pray at home and rarely attend the mosque, particularly in the countryside).

'You have to be clean when you pray. You have to wash your hands, feet and face thoroughly,' she explains with the enthusiasm of a neophyte. 'It's best not to pray during your period. It's hard to be clean then, even for a little while. I tried once and washed myself several times a day, but I just couldn't do it. It's better to just make up for missed prayers later.'

Aishat takes off her trousers and even her underwear in order to be sure, as she explains, that she is not wearing anything dirty. She pulls on a black bag with red polka dots that covers all the naked parts on the lower half of her body. She covers her head in a floral scarf. Only her face and hands are left uncovered. We quietly step out of the room so as not to disturb Aishat, but she gestures for us to stay and watch her pray.

'Don't touch the Qur'an!' Aishat interrupts her prayers when she sees us take it off the shelf. 'That is a holy book that may only be touched by Muslims! Even menstruating women aren't supposed to touch it!'

From Aishat's constant comments on our behaviour or alleged promiscuity I gained an impression that in her eyes we were simply 'unclean'. The only thing we could do to change this state of affairs would be to accept Islam, which we were fervently encouraged to do at least several times each day. We were 'unclean' as foreigners, as followers of a non-Muslim faith and hence as people who have intercourse while menstruating and who eat such 'filth' as pork (which is probably forbidden not for health reasons but because of its ritual uncleanliness. The proscription was probably borrowed from earlier cultures in which pigs were sacrificed to the gods and could not be touched or eaten by normal people, who would even be made 'unclean' by coming into contact with swine). But it was not only the ritual 'cleanliness' and 'uncleanliness' that bothered Aishat.

Aishat's watchful eye notices our every misstep, such as forgetting to wash our hands before eating, or even clumsily removing our shoes at the threshold, an activity that requires surprising skill if one is rushed to let the next person through while taking off anything other than slippers. 'Don't stand in front of the house in stocking feet! You'll track dirt inside!' she yelled every time we came in.

We felt uneasy at being rebuked like small kids or intruders and puzzled at the same time.

It would appear that Aishat is obsessed with cleanliness. But even with all understanding and thankfulness for the couple for hosting us, it was hard not to notice that our sheets were dotted with greyish-brown stains, that glasses have been reused several times, dishes rinsed in the filthy dishwater, while the toilet didn't even have a hole. It was a stable with a plank placed across an enormous puddle of excrement. How right was Mary Douglas in arguing there is no absolute category of dirt, one that can be measured with a microscope or quantified in terms of bacteria;[3] what we call dirty is simply a disturbance of the order we are accustomed to. We saw dirt on our host's glasses and sheets and in the litter floating in the canyon. Aishat and many other locals may not see 'our dirt' or consider it important, while we found it strange that she made a point of blowing her nose or changing her underwear before praying or not letting us in the mosque because of menstruation.

* * *

That night, once again, the moon was not seen in the cloudy sky, but the holiday was nevertheless announced. Aishat packs pouches of rice into a bag.

'They're for the poor,' she explains. 'Every Muslim is required to hand out food today.'

On the day in which they break fast, before the ceremonial morning prayers, the villagers give out *zakat al-fitr*. This can take the form of money (the customary amount is equal to the cost of feeding one adult for one day) or food products such as grain or rice. On this day everyone is expected to give charity, regardless of age (fathers pay or hand out *zakat* for their children). *Zakat al-fitr* is given to the poor and needy so that they may celebrate the end of Ramadan just as the more fortunate do. 'Wahhabis' are said to pay *zakat al-fitr* to their 'brothers in the forest' (i.e. militants), who wage holy war against the infidels (jihadists are one of seven categories of people who may be given *zakat*). But do they? We don't dare to ask.

The visiting starts. Children come first, making the rounds from house to house with shopping bags, collecting chocolates, crisps and sweets. They rarely come inside, as they are always in a hurry to find out what the neighbours have in store for them. Once given nuts and dried apricots, today children receive several full bags of sweets of all sorts.

After the children comes time for the men, who arrive to heavily laden tables. 'Wahhabis' must serve guests two days in a row; after all, they can't violate the rules of hospitality over a difference of views. This is a day when hosts pull out all the stops. Alcohol is not served or consumed (it has long been banned in the village, and anyone caught drinking may be banished from the community). Neighbours come in, exchange wishes, sit down for a bite to eat and move on to the next in a long line of houses. As they leave, men are given socks by the woman of the house, while females receive hand towels or chocolates.

After noon *salah*, the men visit the cemetery together to pray for the dead (this is not practised by local 'Wahhabis', who shun the veneration of ancestors). It is then that the women pay each other visits, sharing long conversations without expecting clean glasses or quick service from their friends and relatives. The holiday slowly comes to an end.

No one says a word to us about dirt during the holiday. Such days involve the suspension of rules; it is a time when certain things may be turned upside down. Houses may be entered in shoes, men sit down to eat with women (who still wait on them). The rich and poor, 'Wahhabis' and non-Wahhabis, the powerful and the weak all welcome each other into their homes and share gifts. Everyone is equal during the holiday.

As dawn breaks, the only things left to remind us of yesterday's holiday are the sweet wrappers littering the streets of the *aul*. We help Aishat clean up around the house. Bags of rubbish and scraps are thrown over a cliff outside the village. The creek below carries away the bottles, watermelon rinds, Snickers wrappers and crisp packets. In a few hours, if they don't snag on a branch or rock, they will end up in the Chirkeysk GES.

10

ABDURAKHMAN

'Perestroika', 'Glasnost' and 'Democracy'. Neon signs on the rooftops of three Khrushchev-era apartment blocks date back to when people still believed in those slogans. Up close, the apartment buildings resemble garden sheds stacked one on top of the other. The façade decorated with fading, Samarkand-style mosaics is dotted with windows in a jumble of styles: large and small, plastic, and even round. The inhabitants hoard seemingly random items on their balconies: a door to a Lada, a chair that's missing a leg, refrigerators and mouldy rugs. Some flats have unfinished additions, known as *dostroyki*, built on to the sides of the buildings. These do-it-yourself apartment expansions are a local solution to the housing shortage. In most cases, a wall on the first floor will be torn down and a room or two added outside the building. And if the upstairs neighbours agree to chip in for a better roof, they can build an addition on top of that one. Some of the braver apartment owners build their own expansions on the seventh or even eleventh floors without waiting for their downstairs neighbours. When the first cracks begin to appear, the delicate construction can be propped up with a steel pipe, the bottom of which is sunk a few feet into the ground.

A few stray, long-haired cats bask on the benches in front of the building. The felines are a cross between the 'local breed' and the Persian cats once fashionable in the USSR. They are spoiled, well-fed and rarely harassed by dogs. The latter—abandoned by their Russian owners, who fled the republic fearing the outbreak of war—were rounded up by the police and killed in courtyards and playgrounds in the nineties.

We enter the building marked 'Perestroika'. The damp, musty air inside reeks of cat urine. The elevator won't budge until we deposit 20 kopecks into its coin slot.

Abdurakhman, still half asleep, greets us at the door. The smell of freshness hits our nostrils. With new panelling, couches and an enormous sofa that takes up half the living room, his apartment looks like it has just undergone what is locally known as a *yevroremont*—a thorough, 'European-style' renovation, just like on TV. The door to an old Minsk refrigerator stands in the corner. Abdurakhman is too sentimental to part with all the stickers he once brought home from Europe.

Abdurakhman is the editor of one of Daghestan's few independent newspapers. He writes about the republic's problems and human rights violations, and levels careful criticism against politicians and other corrupt groups. He has lately been receiving death threats with growing frequency. Annoyed politicians warn him to stop publishing 'nonsense' about them, 'or else'. Other 'well-wishing' people remind him that he might have to pay a heavy price for his sharp comments about the police and the 'Wahhabis'. Then there are those who suspect he might be a spy, since his newspaper is partially funded by an American foundation. To make matters worse, Abdurakhman travels around 'enemy' states in the West, and is sometimes visited by friends from Europe, who allegedly come to Daghestan to 'snoop around'. Just to be safe, he avoids long telephone conversations and is careful not to use certain words. He changes his email addresses every so often as a security measure. His sister has advised him to have a new armoured front door put in.

We fear that our prolonged presence could only get him in more trouble. Our visit three years before brought the FSB down on his (and our) head. Or rather, we were paid a visit. Arsen, a tall, polite man dressed in a smart suit, showed up in the evening 'just to chat'. He introduced himself as a 'university representative for foreign students'. We talked about life, foreigners and the purpose of our visit. A bottle of Żubrówka,[1] which the officer took a liking to, salvaged the situation. Arsen must not have had many opportunities to demonstrate his 'revolutionary vigilance'. Foreigners remain a rare sight in Makhachkala.

* * *

One might easily forget that Makhachkala is situated by the sea, were it not for the humid, dusty wind. The mood is nothing like that that of Black Sea resorts. Nor are there any fried-fish eateries like those found along the Baltic coast. What self-respecting highlander would eat such filth? Even the sturgeon and its expensive black caviar have not found their way on to local menus. It's somewhat of a paradox that the city, with its large and important port, faces away from the sea. Highlanders have always kept their distance from the shores. The low-lying plains were once a constant target of attack for marauding Huns, Persians, Arabs and Turks. Safety could only be found in the inaccessible mountains. Another, and perhaps more important, reason why the lowlands were avoided were the abundant mosquitoes inhabiting the marshy land, spreading many diseases, particularly malaria.

Modern-day Makhachkala is the successor of a nineteenth-century Russian military settlement, later transformed into the port town of Port Petrovsk. Soviet authorities quickly changed the tsarist name, taking the local suffix -*kala* (*kale* being the Turkish word for 'castle') and adding a politically appropriate root derived from the name of one of Daghestan's most famous Bolsheviks, Makhach Dakhadaev. The result was one of many such invented toponyms coined in the Soviet Union, including Kaliningrad, Kirovakan, Leninabad and Kolkhozabad.

To the European eye, Makhachkala differs little from hundreds of other medium-sized Russian cities; there's a *ploshchad*, or square, a statue of Lenin (with one hand optionally raised in salute), *marshrutka*s and a hotel called 'Leningrad'. But step out of the Soviet-style downtown area, and you enter a whole different Makhachkala—one with an almost Middle Eastern atmosphere, complete with mosques, Islamic stores and *chaikhana*s (teahouse). Stores remain open well into the night, along with kebab stands, tiny open-air markets, saunas and, until recently, unofficial casinos posing as 'gaming establishments'. Haphazardly built stalls and booths and crumbling apartment buildings buttressed with illegal additions mix with modern shops and several-story mansions. 'New Daghestanis' (the local counterpart of 'New Russians') protect themselves, their families and their wealth by hiding behind 10-foot electrified fences and bulletproof windows—until the day comes when someone takes revenge for an insult, the death of a brother or stolen money. Houses are erected helter-skelter, even in the middle of the road. One consequence is that the number of dead-end streets in the city continues to rise. These new cul-de-sacs can then be renamed (for the right price) in honour of a grandfather, local poet, brother-in-law, a widely respected mafia boss or a recently gunned-down businessman—a new local way of remembering the dead.

The result is that Makhachkala exists in a state of architectural chaos, at least from our European perspective, which sees space as an ordered structure with a clearly defined centre, designed with the viewer in mind. The city's intellectual class complains of the ubiquitous illegal construction, chaos and disorder. Perhaps it is actually just an unwitting destruction of the old, imposed Soviet order?

* * *

The doorbell rings. In comes Efik with his wife Tania, an English teacher. They carry an enormous watermelon and a 1.5 litre plastic bottle of Derbent beer. Ruslan, nicknamed by Abdurakhman 'a Bahá'í' for his attraction towards this faith, follows soon after. Next come Rizvan, recalled always by our host when it comes to women and Armen (who recently bought an infant from a teenage mother). And finally Gasan, with a shopping bag full of tomatoes and a chicken. He pulls a bottle of cognac out of his coat.

The guests share stories and gossip revealing little by little their everyday concerns and cares. Rizvan complains that his brother lost a newly bought position at the prosecutor's office when the prosecutor general who 'hired' him was killed. Not having spent a full six months on the job, the relative didn't even manage to break even (the customary price for a post is usually the equivalent of six months' pay). Armen boasts about his new daughter. He has bought a newborn infant from a young woman who didn't want the child and didn't have an abortion within the reasonable time period. They didn't arrange it officially. 'Why pay bribes? Get all relatives involved? She didn't want all that. She was young, you understand.' Gasan is saving up to cover the cost of his daughter's 'free' university education in Makhachkala. If he can't afford it, he'll send her to Moscow. 'It's cheaper that way,' he says. Rizvan quietly admits that his relative has joined the police—a cause of shame for the family.

The party is soon in full swing. The chicken quickly disappears, leaving pickled green tomatoes, Moscow salad with herring and beets, and Kizlyar cognac. The guests hold stormy debates, argue with each other, tell jokes and raise toasts: *Za lyubov! Za devushki!* (To love! To girls) To peace on earth and to the amity of nations. As our friends insist, the entire world should follow the example of Daghestan, which, supposedly, has never seen inter-ethnic conflict, and whose nationalities live as one, big, loving family.

* * *

It was already well past sunset when the muezzin's call to prayer rang out from the soaring minarets of the grand new mosque that had recently been completed just a few blocks away.

'I'm an atheist but I don't go out on the balcony and shout "There is no God" at five in the morning! Why should they? Religion is a private matter'—says Efik.

'What could you possibly know about God, Efik?' Abdurakhman interrupted the atheist's theological musings to pour another glass of Stolichnaya.

As the night wore on, the guests gravitated toward the smoke-filled kitchen. A heated discussion had been going on for hours over the essence of God, mortality and eternity, faith and faithlessness and the meaning of life. Latin phrases were exchanged, Pushkin and Akhmatova were recited, and the ballads of Okudzhava and Vysotsky were sung.

They are the crème de la crème of the Daghestani—and Russian—intelligentsia. They believe in democracy and Europe. Abdurakhman, Efik, Tania: each of them had their five minutes under Gorbachev and the early Yeltsin administration. First they placed their trust in the former ruler's promise of socialism with a human face—a Soviet Union with freedom of speech and elements of true democracy. Later, when what they thought would be an eternal empire collapsed, they decided that true democracy and civil society were possible in Russia, and that the West was not an enemy to the Russians, but their natural ally. They believed that breaking with the legacy of communism—in their eyes a criminal regime—was a prerequisite for progress. The fall of the Iron Curtain was a blessing to them. They could finally visit Paris, Rome and Berlin. They could breathe freely in Europe, the continent they considered their home. They spent those years having heated debates in private kitchens, in the relatively free press and TV of the time, and at all sorts of conferences and meetings. They quarrelled, they argued, they watched as Yanayev attempted his 1991 coup,[2] and as Yeltsin ordered Russian troops to open fire on the White House.[3] And they were satisfied, unlike most of the population, which hated Gorbachev, the man who 'destroyed' the Soviet Union, and the drunken president who 'sold out' and 'brought shame' upon Russia.

* * *

The time of the perestroika and democracy came to an end much sooner in Daghestan than in the rest of Russia—even before Putin and the security services in which he began his career took over the Kremlin. After the collapse of the USSR, Moscow was too involved in its own affairs to intervene in Daghestan, or in the entire North Caucasus for that matter. The spectre of ethnic conflict loomed over the republic. Dozens of national movements sprung up, each raising mutually conflicting demands. Kumyk and Nogai leaders called for the deportation of Avars and Dargins from the former's land, while Chechens supported the recreation of the Aukhovsky District, dissolved in 1944 with the expulsion of Chechens to Central Asia. Meanwhile, Lezgins wanted the Azeri lands that were inhabited by members of their ethnic group to be incorporated into Daghestan. On top of that, war broke out in 1994 in neighbouring Chechnya, several organisations began calling for the transformation of Daghestan into an Islamic state and organised crime flourished to unprecedented levels.

Surprisingly enough, no revolution took place in Daghestan. The local intelligentsia attributes that fact to the 'instinct for compromise' that is believed to be so deeply ingrained in Daghestani society. Split into dozens of independent city-states, khanates and free *jamaat*s before the Russian conquest, Daghestani society had no choice but to develop mechanisms that would allow its members to avoid conflict and lead stable lives. They learned to compromise. Had that skill and habit survived the years of tsarist and Soviet rule and kicked in during the nineties? At that time, Daghestani nations, groups of influence, informal associations, clans and *jamaat*s were capable of reaching an agreement, and carved up their spheres of influence in a manner that precluded the outbreak of civil war. It worked well for a while.

Looking at the modern Daghestani political system, one cannot help but wonder if a revolution isn't just what the republic needs. Post-communist diehards rule the republic alongside the mafia, with plenty of mutual back-scratching. This is likely the most fitting summary of how the government works. Daghestan's communist nomenklatura never ceded power. Magomedali Magomedov, an old party apparatchik and cunning political actor, simply became the head of the State Council in 1991—the highest level of government in Daghestan prior to 2006, when the office of president was created. Subsequent leaders of Daghestan: Magomedsalam Magomedov (son of Magomedali Magomedov), Mukhu Aliyev and a current Head of the Republic of Daghestan, Ramazan Abdulatipov, were also a part of the Soviet nomenklatura. The leaders were nevertheless forced to share influence with power- and money-hungry 'young wolves'—unfulfilled Komsomol activists and leaders of ethnic-based criminal organisations, such as the famous mafia boss and racketeer Gadzhi Makhachev. He went on to lead the Avars alongside Basayev and dreamed of an 'independent Daghestan', before switching his slogan to 'Daghestan: With Russia Forever' and fighting back against Chechen raids in 1999 with fellow racketeers. An effective and unscrupulous criminal with good 'political muscle', Makhachev was eventually awarded a medal and a chair in the Russian Duma.[4] The careers of Sagidpasha Umakhanov, an influential head of Khasavyurt and Sagid Murtuzaliev, a head of Kizlyar region have taken similar paths.

In the Daghestani system of government, an armed personal gang is a fundamental political tool. Any self-respecting Daghestani politician, from ministers down to local government leaders, has tens or hundreds of thugs ready to follow orders at a moment's notice. This might simply involve 'explaining' contentious issues to rivals, but should one refuse to understand, the henchmen may resort to more drastic measures: threatening to put a bullet in his head, take an uncle hostage or beat up a brother-in-law. And if that doesn't help, a car bomb can be planted. Of course, the thugs don't wait on full alert every day. Only the big shots have private armies and security details at their disposal. Small fry have to turn to their clans or family villages to round up an army when necessary. But everything has a price: in exchange for supporting an important relative—and assuming the risks that come with it—they expect help with 'everyday' problems such as buying a job or driver's licence, passing an exam or securing a hospital bed. A refusal would spell the end of his political career.

* * *

A few have tried to change this 'system'—to reform it and change the existing balance of power, either for ideological reasons or because they missed the first power-grab of the early nineties. None of them are alive today. There are also hardly any Caucasus Emirate fighters left. They also tried to change the 'evil' political system and introduce a 'just' one with help of Sharia, but in the end they became a part of the local political struggles. They were killing some representatives of the system, yet acting as hitmen for others. Politics in Daghestan is serious business. No one wastes time on discussions, debates, smear campaigns, libel lawsuits or impeachment. The hitmen are paid and a press release is prepared, stating that Mr so-and-so has been killed in an attack carried out by Islamic militants. Everyone knows who ordered the hit, but they keep quiet, as they themselves are, or soon will be, guilty of the same crime. The use of paid assassins isn't even considered a big faux-pas. It's a widely accepted political tactic.

Dozens of Daghestani politicians have been killed by sniper fire and remotely triggered bombs. Explosives were used to assassinate two consecutive ministers of nationality policy, Magomedsalikh Gusayev and Zagir Arukhov, both rumoured to have been potential candidates for president of Daghestan.

Magomed and Nadirshah Khachilayev—leaders of the Lak national movement and later proponents of Sharia law in Daghestan—met the same fate. Nadir wasn't even saved by his former position as deputy to the Duma. He stepped out of line by questioning the status quo; he asked too much, and thus had to be killed.

Meanwhile, some Daghestani politicians, such as Makhachkala ex-Mayor Said Amirov, have been extraordinarily lucky. For a while. Amirov has survived over a dozen assassination attempts: his car has been blown up, he has been shot at with a Kalashnikov rifle and many snipers have tried to take him down, to no avail. Amirov is still alive, though confined to a wheelchair. His political career has come to an end only in 2013. He lost a battle over influence with Ramazan Abdulatipov, a leader from a different clan and a current Head of the Republic of Daghestan. Amirov was arrested and sentenced to life imprisonment. Lust for power and money seems stronger than fear and common sense. And what does Moscow have to say about all this? The capital wants just one thing: relative peace. Federal authorities are willing to look the other way as long as the bombings, shootings and other acts of violence committed in Daghestan are kept 'within reasonable limits'. It is only from time to time that the Kremlin interferes or like in the case of Amirov, supports one clan against another. For Moscow officials, Daghestanis are 'a people of their word', unlike Chechens, who have 'the audacity' to open fire at each other in front of the very walls of the Kremlin and chase each other around Moscow in SUVs with tinted windows, shooting Kalashnikov rifles. Daghestanis take care of their affairs at home.

Some Russian minister or presidential envoy will occasionally show a modicum of interest in Daghestan. He will send a commission to the republic, draw up an alarming report, call for immediate action on the part of the Kremlin and overplay the threat of Islamic revolution. But after a month or two, everything goes back to normal. As long as there's no war—that's the only concern for the Russian authorities.

* * *

The party is slowly winding down. Guests begin to head home, stumbling down the dark staircase and tripping over knee-deep potholes in front of the building. At dawn, they will return to their mundane routines in a world where intellectuals have no say. They can only sit in their kitchens and debate the essence of God, sipping cognac and snacking on pickles. Or they can discuss the quasi-democratic world of the late eighties and early nineties that is unlikely ever to come back.

Abdurakhman and his circle of friends are 'oddballs' and outsiders in Daghestan. There's no room for 'weakling intellectuals' in Putin's Russia, much less in Daghestan. If things continue down this path, there will be soon only three categories of people in the republic: the criminals in power, the Islamic militants in the forest and the easily manipulated masses between them, hostages in a life-and-death struggle. There will be no place for bookish nerds.

To Daghestani intellectuals, contact with Europe, with people from Europe, is a breath of fresh air; a Europe that knows nothing, nor wants to know anything, of their existence. Daghestan doesn't meet EU norms. Officials at the French and German embassies in Moscow have probably a separate pile for visa applications submitted by people with names like 'Magomed Gadzhiyev', born in places like 'Makhachkala, Daghestan'. Criminals and potential refugees need not apply. Unless they can produce an invitation, bearing half a dozen official stamps, from some country behind the Schengen curtain, along with proof of funds, employment evidence, insurance for their entire period of stay and, ideally, visas from previous trips to the European Union, proving they have no intention of applying for refugee status as soon as they arrive in Warsaw or Vienna. Only then is there a good chance that the disgruntled clerk who collects the visa forms from the mob crowding in front of the consulate gate will—in pursuance of some obscure European Commission directive—toss the application on to the 'approved' pile, giving the applicant hope of reaching Terespol (a small town in Poland on the border with Belarus), the 'gate of Europe', where a customs officer, irritated at working the night shift to protect the European frontier, will ask in broken Russian: 'Where are you going? Do you have money? What's the purpose of your visit?' before finally placing that coveted stamp in the passport.

Russian officials (and their Ukrainian, Georgian and Azeri counterparts), many living off corruption, are usually given priority treatment. They fly to Brussels to attend EU-funded seminars on fighting corruption and fostering civil society. Europe spends hundreds of millions of euros on bolstering civil society and personal freedom in the East, deceiving itself about its meaningful contribution to the cause of democracy in the region, without stopping to consider whether it has achieved anything besides lining the coffers of numerous professional non-governmental organisations whose cunning fundraisers hold one event after another, producing an endless stream of 'democratic' projects and expensive brochures read by no one. Perhaps it would do more good by letting Daghestanis and other 'barbarians' cross the border freely and meet people from our part of the continent?

11

SAUNAS

'A young boy came up to me on the street and said, "It's people like you that are going to bring the world to an end,"' Aminat, a twenty-year-old acquaintance of Abdurakhman recalls. 'He was talking about my tight jeans. He looked at me with contempt and walked away, saying that soon they would start shooting at all the immodestly dressed girls!'

'Muslims! Awake! Do you want your children to become gays, prostitutes, and lesbians tomorrow? Do you want them to teach you how to live a godless life? Awaken from your slumber, Muslims! Look around! What has Russia done with our bold, masculine nation of pure hearts? They have taken our men and turned them into arrogant and boastful drunks and adulterers; they have turned our women into lustful girls no different from the infidels!'

This statement was posted sometime in 2009 on the website of the Caucasian Emirate[1] but nobody paid attention to it, until a few days in August 2009 when a rumour spread throughout the city that militants would be hunting down 'half-naked' girls. The attackers were said to be on the lookout for any number of items, including fashionable above the knee skirts, pencil skirts with long slits, stretch denim, sheer low-cut blouses or, even worse, belly tops (which expose a part of the body regarded as highly intimate and unsuitable for display outside the bedroom). All of these disappeared from the streets of Makhachkala, as did the several hundred dollar dresses worn by Daghestani women as both professional and wedding attire, and which serve to emphasise the wearer's social status and arouse envy among girlfriends. Not everyone bought into the rumours, but just to be on the safe side, girls went through their wardrobes, pulling out long dresses and donning headscarves they hadn't worn since their last visits to their grandmothers in the mountains. They gave a wide berth to any places where they risked being spotted by friends. Some preferred not to leave the house at all. There were more rumours about a girl who had been threatened with a gun for wearing what was considered too short a skirt. She was said to have run home and did not venture outside for a whole week. Another girl was allegedly chased and threatened by a band of bullies who were apparently taking advantage of the general atmosphere of panic. Even Daghestani branches of Russian companies such as Gazprom imposed a dress code that was almost in line with Islamic rulings on proper attire, requiring women to wear a modest, 'feminine' outfit consisting of ankle-length skirts and long-sleeved blouses. Whether the requirement was intended to improve workplace discipline or simply avoid confrontation with the militants was never explained. Meeting up with friends at a café was out of the question, as was going out to clubs in the evening. The streets were deserted after dark. There was something in the air.

* * *

'A recent attack by the mujahideen of the Daghestani Front's Central Sector on a sauna in Temir-Khan-Shur (formerly Buynaksk) resulted in the death of eleven prostitutes: four moral prostitutes wearing the uniform of Iblis [the Devil] and seven physical prostitutes without uniforms. There was no time during the attack to discern between moral and physical prostitutes. The mujahideen destroyed them both. The former kill Muslims, while the latter help them unwind after a hard day of "work." Both of them hate Islam and purity—they hate pure Muslims,' wrote news websites associated with the Caucasian Emirate, reporting on attacks on a police station and sauna that took place on 13 August 2009.

The official media described the events as just another act of banditry; independent outlets mentioned the ties between the police and prostitution rings, while the unofficial Islamic media hailed it as a victory in the fight against promiscuity. That the saunas are just a front for brothels is common knowledge—even among children, and especially the children at municipal school number 18, the basement of which housed an (after-school) sauna for over a year. As the entrepreneurial principal later explained, 'The men were just there to take a bath.' No one was particularly surprised by the murder of the police officers in Buynaksk. The event was just another in a series of similar incidents that had taken place over the years. Policemen—beat cops, traffic cops and police chiefs—died every day. Nor did anyone shed a tear over the death of the prostitutes. Death wasn't the issue; the topic itself was approached calmly. The question that cropped up time and again was: how could the prostitutes be Daghestani? How could our girls end up in places like that? As it turned out, the girls murdered in the attack had been natives of the republic. 'Our girls? No, that's impossible. Daghestan is a Muslim republic, and our women are respectable.' 'The saunas only employ Russians and Ukrainians,' people said with ever-decreasing conviction. A consensus was ultimately reached when it occurred to someone to pin the 'immorality' on Daghestani women who had come home from Turkmenistan in the nineties.[2] There were various local explanations why girls would choose to work at saunas: 'odd' customs, the lack of relatives or other source of supervision, or simply poverty (the fact that Daghestani jewellers in Turkmenistan were famously wealthy was conveniently overlooked).

Meanwhile, the press ran increasingly bold and frequent scandal pieces and rumours that weren't quite as easy to dismiss. It was an open secret among students that a 'list of girls' was being passed around the university campus. Compiled by local authorities, the list 'accidentally' fell into the hands of students, who then made it available for a small fee. Men who acquired a copy used it to blackmail the girls on the list, demanding money or sex in exchange for not revealing the truth to their families. According to another story that spread throughout the city, a man took his eighteen-year-old son on a trip to a Makhachkala sauna so that he might gain experience and prowess and avoid embarrassment in front of his friends. To the surprise of all involved, the man was greeted by his own daughter. The shocked father killed the girl and then committed suicide.

'He was a real Caucasian man. He did the right thing. He couldn't but kill her. It's a Caucasian tradition!'—said my friend.

'Hey, but what about father and son? Is it also a Caucasian tradition to take one's sons to a sauna organised for sexual relations?'—I wanted to ask, but ultimately didn't.

The only question that was raised was how a 'girl from a good home' could have ended up in such a place? How could Daghestani girls from mountain *auls* brought up on the strict mountain *adats*, taught to be obedient to her father and brothers and severely punished for the slightest transgressions (coming home past curfew, walking around the village with a boyfriend or 'immodest' dress, not to mention premarital sex) end up in saunas?

The saunas typically attracted young girls from the villages. They would arrive in the city with a sense of inferiority, their modest clothing betraying their origin, social status and poverty. All around they saw dresses worth thousands of dollars, the latest cellphones and people enjoying casual, fun lives. They were tempted by wages of twenty dollars an hour. The easiest prey for pimps were girls who were not accepted into university, for lack of knowledge or, more commonly, money. They shuddered at the prospect of returning to the countryside. Other country girls trying their luck in the city ended up in saunas after answering classified ads for 'well-paid jobs with a free apartment'. They would be hired as waitresses or cooks in brothels and, eventually, required to perform additional services. Not wanting to return to the mountains, they gave in. Parents, upon learning of their daughters' occupation, would often disown them and break off all ties. Without any other way to make a living and with little hope of marrying, the girls remained in the saunas—alone and with no one to turn to.

'I bought freedom for one of those girls,' says Valera, Abdurakhman's acquaintance. 'Raisa was eighteen years old. She was from a small village. She had been doing it for two years, and she was ready to commit suicide. I paid them. I found her a job. She had a modest income. But nothing changed. She just couldn't lead a normal life anymore. A year later, she was gone, without even so much as a thank you. They say she left for the United Arab Emirates. It was like a deadly addiction.'

* * *

'It's about time we got rid of those saunas! And girls should start dressing more modestly, too! Like Muslims, not Russians! Who would want to marry a girl like that?' 'They've spoiled this nation! Someone has to clean this mess up!' Suddenly women and their 'morality' have become a 'topic of concern' not only to militants but also steadfast Stalinists who hold to their views on the impeccable morality of Soviet society (and who wish to see in every woman a mother bearing children for the benefit of the nation), and 'traditionalists' who tearfully dream their sons will grow up to be virile *dzhigit*s, and their daughters proud Caucasian maidens.

The militants' intent to destroy the saunas and other 'dens of iniquity' won the silent support of the people. If these establishments could not be dealt with peacefully through legal means, or even through blackmail—by making undercover video recordings and threatening to air the footage on television—then 'somebody had to clean things up'. Things had recently been 'cleaned up' in the republic of Ingushetia, where constant militant attacks on saunas had led to their complete disappearance from the streets of Nazran a few years before. Chechen President Ramzan Kadyrov had also managed to take care of the problem. Had the time come for a 'moral' revolution in Daghestan?

* * *

Interest in the sauna attacks gradually waned. Miniskirts and fishnet tights came back into fashion. As for the saunas, it was business as usual. Their owners merely rebranded them as 'spas', 'sports centres' or even 'cultural centres'; others were now called steam baths or banyas. Even the word 'hotel' lost some of its original meaning—a change that can potentially lead to misunderstandings among unaware foreigners. Just to be on the safe side, we recommend avoiding hotels with exotic-sounding names, and instead choosing one of the ubiquitous Soviet-sounding *gostinitsas*, such as Leningrad, Druzhba or Komsomolets.

Nevertheless, something besides the names of the brothels has changed. By raising women issues, the militants have gained confidence, sensing silent public support for their cause. University students and other young people began speaking openly about their sympathies, not just for the peaceful Salafis but also for the 'forest brothers'. They no longer hesitated to skip classes in order to attend Friday prayers. They began to voice their contempt for the government, seeing a state ruled by Allah as the only path to justice. The 'sauna incident' showed the militants that they do enjoy significant, albeit silent, social support, and that they are a force to be reckoned with. They began proselytising openly, and even targeted some unexpected groups.

'Accept Islam! Trust us—Islam is the path to salvation!' two bearded men explained loudly and confidently to a police officer in downtown Makhachkala. He, as a friend of Abdurakhman recalls, seemed somewhat startled but listened obediently.

12

IF I EVER WERE A SULTAN

Larisa, an acquaintance of Abdurakhman, works at the Makhachkala Philharmonic. She is a college graduate with a degree in music. She comes from an urban family and rarely visits her relatives in the countryside, preferring instead the fast-paced lifestyle of the city, where all her friends live. She sings in an ethno-pop band with her colleagues from the philharmonic. With their operatic voices, the all-female quartet quickly became a favourite among Makhachkala youth. They now play concerts and perform at weddings all across the Caucasus.

Larisa fell pregnant. The father, Rasul, is married with children. 'He didn't pressure her into getting an abortion. He tries to be a pious Muslim'—explains a friend of Larisa. They were married in a traditional Islamic ceremony, known as a *nikah*, at home in the presence of witnesses and an imam. The wedding was a low-key affair, with no pageantry or reception. They didn't see the need. Their bride's parents did not oppose the marriage.

'After all, she is over thirty years old'—says Larisa's friend. 'And this way, she has a baby and they have the same rights as Rasul's other wife and children—according to Sharia law at least.'

Larisa's new husband is a businessman who owns several cars and a house in downtown Makhachkala. He gave her an apartment as a wedding gift. He supports her and takes her shopping in his late-model Jeep. 'It seems to be working out between them. He treats them both the same,' explains Larisa's friend.

* * *

To many, polygamy is the most recognisable 'feature' of Islam. It is a controversial issue in the West, one that provokes frequent criticism and is a source of misunderstandings about Islam. It 'legitimises' the branding of Muslims as 'barbarians' who oppress their women. Meanwhile, Muslims themselves have serious doubts about the institution, a fact frequently overlooked.

> And if you fear that you will not deal justly with the orphan girls, then marry those that please you of [other] women, two or three or four. But if you fear that you will not be just, then [marry only] one or those your right hand possesses.
>
> Qur'an, Sura 4 (an-Nisa), verse 3
>
> He who has two wives and is not just between them, he will come on the Day of Resurrection with one of his sides fallen.
>
> Abu Dawood 2133

The Qur'an permits men to take up to four wives, while at the same time requiring each of them to be treated equally. Many see this condition as impossible to fulfil and thus regard polygamy as de facto forbidden. Those who have no issue with the provision must still fulfil several additional requirements, the most important of which is that the potential polygamist must have the means to provide for all his wives and children—an insurmountable hurdle to the average owner of a tiny Khrushchev-era apartment. It is also forbidden for the wives to share a bed, as they are required to live separately. 'It's for the very wealthy, just another whim, alongside trained tigers and crocodiles guarding their downtown homes: just another way of outdoing the "New Russians."' Poor Daghestanis can at least 'take comfort' in knowing that with more wives comes more trouble, as in the famous Russian song from the film *Kidnapping, Caucasian Style*.[1]

> *If I ever were a sultan, I would have three wives.*
> And surrounded by three beauties I would thrive.
> On the other hand again, if I went that far,
> I would also have three mothers-in-law
> Yes, to have many wives seems to be all right,
> But it looks very bad on the other side.
>
> There's a question for us sultans, most important in life:
>
> How many wives to have, three wives or one wife?
> And the answer to this question, clear as a day:
> If I ever were a sultan, single I would stay.

While there are numerous stories and anecdotes about polygamy passed around in contemporary Caucasian folklore, few inhabitants of the region choose to share relationships with two, three or four other people.

Although one can trace the Islamic tradition of polygamy back to the time of Muhammad (who had several wives of his own), mini-harems are a relatively new phenomenon in the Caucasus. Polygamy never took root in Daghestan, despite the centuries-long presence of Islam in the region, and was rarely practised openly, as it conflicted with the local *adat*s. Polygamy was practically unheard of in neighbouring Chechnya until Soviet times—1944, to be exact—when Stalin decided to deport the entire population of the Caucasian republic to the steppes of Kazakhstan and Kyrgyzstan. Many never survived the journey, dying of hunger and exhaustion along the way. Faced with the imminent extinction of the Chechen people, the nation's Islamic leaders encouraged men to take additional wives and bear greater numbers of children. Polygamy made a comeback in Chechnya in the nineties, when the post-war gender imbalance and religious revival made the practice more acceptable.

While Sharia law may have had a strong influence on family life—with such rituals as weddings, funerals and divorces all conducted according to Islamic law—it never succeeded in fully replacing the deeply rooted, and often conflicting, *adat*s. For instance, a man, upon discovering his wife in bed with another man, was within his rights to kill both of them without being guilty of their blood (wives did not enjoy similar rights). But if he were to kill only one of the pair, or kill both of them without having caught them in the act, he would be tried as a murderer. The Qur'an's ruling on actions such as the above is somewhat different, albeit not as severe as is commonly believed. Adultery, when committed by persons not married to others, carries a punishment of 100 lashes, and no fewer than four adult witnesses are required for a conviction. But the Qur'an is not the only source of law in Islam; there is also the Sunnah (from the Arabic word for 'road' or 'path'), which tells of the life and teachings of Muhammad and was written down long after his death. Muslim theologians themselves often have trouble deciding which law takes precedence and how it applies to a given case. Adultery only merits death by stoning according to some interpretations of one of the hadiths.

Sharia law may have taken firmer root in Daghestan than in neighbouring republics, but Daghestanis remained equally conservative in their views on polygamy. The Soviets didn't face any particular resistance in their fight against this particular pre-revolutionary 'holdover', which is not to say that scattered incidents of more or less covert polygamy did not occur; men with more than one wife simply kept quiet about the matter (often while openly boasting about the affairs they had while away on business).

Polygamy became a 'hot' subject of public debate in the nineties. It was presented as an element of the 'tradition' that needed to be revived. 'We have to return to the rules of our faith and live according to Sharia law if we are to find a place for ourselves in the modern world,' some said. Few local Muslims would question the validity of polygamy as 'an institution', and many would even claim its superiority over European family models. Some would support it by arguing that there are 'too many' women in Russia and that 'nobody's women need to be taken care of. Even fewer dare put their words into practice, fearing the social and economic consequences of such a step.

It was also in the nineties that local Shi'ites (who had simply considered themselves Muslims until researchers classified them as such) discovered that Shia Islam permitted them not only to have four wives but also an unlimited number of 'temporary wives'. In relationships of this type, referred to as *nikah mut'ah*, or 'pleasure marriage', a man and woman vow, in the presence of a cleric, to remain husband and wife for a pre-determined period of time, which can be a year, a month, a day or even an hour. Once the contract expires, both parties separate as if they had never been married. Sunnis banned the practice in the seventh century, seeing it as a legalised form of prostitution, the only difference being that any offspring born of the *nikah mut'ah* would be given the same rights as a child born in permanent wedlock, or *nikah* (from the word meaning 'procreation'). The practice is unlikely to have had any significant impact on the lifestyle of Daghestani Shi'ites. Perhaps they've become less shy about flirting with Natashas and Tamaras from Moscow, only to return obediently to their henpecking wives?

* * *

We meet with Larisa in the dressing room at the philharmonic. She has just performed a family themed song to the tune of an ABBA track—the lyrics were required to tie into the slogan 'Daghestan: One Family' proudly displayed on a banner hung above the stage. She has lost weight and tours frequently. Her son is now two years old. Her husband doesn't come around too often. He no longer takes Larisa shopping. He is terrified that his first wife might find out. Makhachkala isn't a large town. They say she's getting suspicious. Does this sound familiar? Perhaps we should take a look around before denouncing polygamy as 'barbarian'.

13

HOW THEY DO IT IN THE CAUCASUS

A pious Muslim should always utter the word *Bismillah* before commencing with any important activity. This includes the deed commonly referred to throughout the Caucasus region as *tuda-siuda*, which can be roughly translated as 'hooking up' (literally 'back and forth'). In theory, *tuda-siuda* is only permitted with one's wife (or wives, if a man is wealthy enough to support more than one). In practice, 'a real' Daghestani *dzhigit* indulges in *tuda-siuda*—not just with his wife—whenever he has the chance. At least that's what he tells his friends. The practice is met with the silent acceptance of society, and even with the implicit approval of some wives. A guy has to get his fun somewhere. Women, on the other hand, have sex exclusively with their (own) husbands. At least that's what they tell their families. A man who only engages in *tuda-siuda* with his own wife, or remains completely abstinent before marriage, is often the subject of endless gossip and suspicion. 'Maybe there's something wrong with him.' 'Maybe he just keeps it hush-hush.' 'Maybe ... No ... We don't have their kind around here. Not like in depraved Western countries. He wouldn't make it home on his own two feet if his friends got whiff of that!' Every 'normal' man is expected to have sex whenever the opportunity arises. Those who do not, inevitably fall into one of three categories: men who can't, gay men and deeply religious Muslims. The last of these reasons is assumed not to apply to abstinent foreigners, who thus fall under the first two labels.

* * *

95

'How do I get to the city centre?' I once asked a taxi driver on my first visit to Makhachkala.

'You can usually find them right here,' replied the cabbie with a lewd grin.

'Find who? What are you talking about?'

'Oh, come on. Don't play dumb. We both know you're talking about *devushki* [girls].'

The people of Daghestan are famous for their hospitality. A host will spare no effort in fulfilling his guest's most secret desires. And what could a guy long for when away on a *komandirovka* (business trip), far from his wife's watchful eye? Daghestani men have no trouble putting two and two together. The question is inevitable: 'Don't you want to try our *devushki*?' (by 'our' he probably meant Russian or Ukrainian, as we were to learn later).

* * *

The situation is starkly different when a man and woman are travelling together. It is immediately assumed that the couple are husband and wife. Questions regarding the size of their family come up first.

'You are husband and wife, right?'

'How many kids do you have?'

'None yet.'

'Why not! You have to start working on that!'

Daghestanis certainly do work hard on it. Families with five or six children are by no means uncommon. The republic's most 'industrious' inhabitants are the Tabasarans, who live in the south, and the Daghestani Chechens. Their families sometimes number up to ten children.

* * *

Women travelling by themselves are a rare sight in the North Caucasus. Daghestani men must watch their tongues in front of the local girls, but have no such qualms when it comes to foreign women. Men in the Caucasus sort women into three categories: local *tselki* (virgins) and married women, local *razvedionki* (as divorcees are called in Russian youth slang) and 'other'. The first always belong to somebody: a husband, a brother, a father or a cousin. A Caucasian man will think twice before making his advances. The prospect of a sound beating is enough to keep him from stepping over the line. The second category will be discussed later. The third have no 'owner' and are considered fair game, especially when found travelling in the Caucasus without a male companion. There is the ubiquitous belief that women from outside the

Caucasus are 'easy' and can be loosened up with a bottle of champagne, some chocolate and a few good pickup lines.

'Hey, babe! Come on, let's go have shashliks in the mountains!'

'Hey, beautiful! How about we go to a restaurant?'

'Don't tell me you're scared! There's nothing to be afraid of!'—I heard now and then. Men in Daghestan seemed fully convinced that any woman who wanders into the Caucasus dreams only of throwing herself into the arms of a dark-haired *dzhigit*. Daghestanis aren't the only ones. Georgians and Armenians have even greater imaginations, and are eager to fulfil the desires of any blue-eyed Slavic girl who crosses their path.

* * *

'There was no sex in the USSR.' Or so claimed Ludmila Nikolaevna Ivanova in a famous 1986 television program, jointly hosted in Leningrad and Boston. Despite its deep Sovietisation and great nostalgia for the former empire, Daghestan seems not to have got the message. Sex is not as taboo a subject there as one would imagine. People discuss details of their intimate lives rather openly, albeit with one minor caveat: women talk to women, and men talk to men (or foreign women).

The pious Daghestani men would ask serious questions with grave looks on their faces, and lecture on the superiority of Islam over all other creeds—even when it comes to intimacy. We learned that a man should shower after sex (and even before, if he is so inclined). Or that sex is forbidden when a woman is suffering from the 'female sickness'. Or that every method of pleasuring one's partner is permitted (halal), except for one (which is haram). All we can say is that vanilla sex is not the only option, and that women in Islam don't always assume an inferior role. Pious Daghestani were eager to offer us their advice on any aspect of *tuda-siuda* regulated by Islam.

Most Daghestani men, however, would rather boast about their—real or imaginary—intimate lives. They would fondly recall the Polish girls they would slip away to when serving on Soviet military bases in Legnica or Stargard Szczeciński. Over a bottle of beer or vodka they would tell dirty jokes and stories about Natashas and Tatianas from Moscow.

In one popular joke, a professor is asked whether it is better to have a wife or a mistress. He replies, 'It is best to have both: your wife thinks you're with your mistress, your mistress thinks you're with your wife, and you get to spend some time in the library.' Daghestanis are nothing like the witty professor. The consumption of books is not a particularly popular pastime in the region, although 90 per cent of local men would agree with the first part of the professor's quip.

Many Daghestani men dream of having a wife at home and a girlfriend (or two) in Moscow or some other Russian city. The wife (preferably of the same ethnicity) would be tasked with child-rearing, washing, cleaning and 'providing' the husband with the necessary social status (unmarried and childless men garner little respect in Daghestan), while the mistress would give him a bit of fun and something to boast about in front of friends. It isn't unheard of for a man to take a Daghestani lover, but 'nothing beats a real Russian woman'. Any Caucasian—even the most steadfast Georgian nationalist—will agree.

In *I am a Chechen!*, German Sadulaev, a resident of St Petersburg and one of Chechnya's most talented contemporary writers, writes that the greatest weapon Russia wields against the Chechens is not the tank, the airplane, nor the armoured personnel carrier, but the Russian woman, against whose charms no Caucasian stands a chance. What is it that makes this secret weapon so effective?

'You know Russians aren't considered any prettier, but they do it like "in films", they know how to play. We are taught all our life to be modest. So we just lay down flat'—one Chechen woman explained. 'But as long as they don't bring over AIDS many women don't mind. At least they let them alone.'

'Russians are easy. Caucasian girls would think twice before entering into a romance'—suggested the other.

Some women do choose to live in extramarital relationships, though. 'You just need to be careful.' A pregnancy, should it occur, is always the female's problem, and the man can only be counted on to pay for the abortion, at the most. The woman is also the one who needs to worry about birth control, a matter that local men consider too petty to concern themselves with, despite the rampant spread of AIDS and sexually transmitted diseases in the North Caucasus. No 'self-respecting' Daghestani man would ever stoop to using a condom; and other methods, even the 'Vatican roulette', don't seem to have caught on.

When it comes to the social perception of informal relationships, men also enjoy a privileged position. The male in such a relationship is regarded as a virile *dzhigit*, while his partner's reputation takes a hit. Thus young women from the North Caucasus who choose to enter into relationships with no prospects of marriage go to great lengths to protect their virginity. This is not to suggest they avoid any *tuda-siuda* whatsoever—they simply have ways around it. If all else fails, a minor operation can always be performed right before the wedding, allowing the bride to fool her groom into thinking he was her first. The only trouble is that the results of the procedure last merely a few days. A suspicious husband can delay consummating the marriage, and—if his doubts turn out to be not unfounded—the woman may be thrown out of the house, leaving her with slim chances of remarrying.

Divorcees get away with informal relationships somewhat easier. Any single woman over the age of thirty is assumed to have been divorced. Young *razvedionki* (divorcees), of which there is no shortage in the Caucasus, are constantly followed by small crowds of admirers who have no intention of starting families. *Tselki* (virgins) are very unlikely to agree to a fleeting romance, not to mention married women. Divorcees are thus a boy's only hope of becoming a man and earning the respect of his peers. They might even learn something along the way. Divorcees, liberated from the shackles of their virginity, are fiercely independent in matters regarding *tuda-siuda*, and have many suitors to choose from. Young *dzhigits* must sometimes offer something in return for a 'visit to the hotel', such as an expensive item of clothing, perfume, an exquisite meal at a restaurant or help in finding employment.

* * *

'Our *dzhigits*! This is all bullshit!'—laughs a forty-year-old Chechen friend of mine. 'One or another with better pick-up lines may actually do it while in Moscow but 90 per cent would just talk about it! Most of them have no money to pay for it and they have sex for the first time with their wives! And even that may not work out! My husband couldn't work it out the first day! He succeeded only on the third! And he was not the only one like that. But they are all *dzhigits* when it comes to stories!'

14

SHAMIL

Butovo metro station, the terminus of the orange line. We're no longer in Moscow, but rather in Podmoskovye, the suburbs. It's a fifteen-minute walk to the subway station, and a one-hour ride into the city from there. Winter is the worst: commuters must trudge through half-thawed slush that piles up faster than the Tajik guest workers can shovel it away. Then there's the harsh, northern wind that howls through the exposed spaces between the newly constructed apartment blocks. But there are bright sides to living this far outside the city. In the summer, parents can take their children to the nearby forest and stroll along the artificial lake, breathe in the fresh air and take a break from Moscow's breakneck pace. 'Did you see them again today?' The family atmosphere is spoiled by the topless sunbathing that goes on at the local beach, right beside the path that leads to the metro station. 'My faith forbids me to peek but it is not easy.'

A modest, small but cosy and neat apartment. As soon as our host finishes his evening prayers in the next room, we sit down to eat from a rug spread out on the floor. Mutton, *plov*, and Daghestani *pierogi*. And then traditional tea and sweets. The excited children show off in front of the guests, keeping them from getting a word in edgeways. It takes Zarina several attempts to put her kids to bed, and we can finally talk.

Because of us (or from Zarina's point of view, thanks to us), Shamil has come home a bit earlier than usual today. He doesn't normally get in until after dark. He has a moment to play with the children before it's time to feed and bathe them. If bedtime goes well, he'll carve out an hour or two to catch up on work in front of the computer. And in the morning it's a quick breakfast, a dash to the metro, an hour on a cramped train and a day of sitting in front of a computer in one of Moscow's analysis centres. With all of that, he still needs to find time for five daily prayers. It's been the same routine, day after day, for two years. There's a bit more time in the summer, when Zarina takes the kids to his parents or in-laws in the Daghestani countryside.

Makhachkala, Yekaterinburg, Makhachkala again, then Cairo and finally back to Moscow. There were trips in the meantime: the United States, Paris, Poland, Abkhazia and the Russian Far East. He's a typical nomad, a vagabond constantly in search of answers, always posing new questions. An eternal wanderer. But there's one journey he hasn't made. One that he's been dreaming about for years, but can't afford just yet. A trip, or rather a pilgrimage, that every Muslim should make at least once in their lives.

'That's just my personality,' admits Shamil, sipping a cup of fragrant tea. 'I just can't sit still for too long. I'm constantly looking for change, for new challenges. Zarina would rather have stability. She has a hard life with me. Someday, *inshallah*, I'll settle down.' But Shamil's constant travels are motivated by more than just personality—at least in recent months.

* * *

It was June 2004. A heavy downpour struck Makhachkala around midday. The streets became rushing rivers and the clogged storm drains spewed their contents back up to the surface. Pedestrians waded through shin-deep. We finally reached the Daghestan Scientific Centre of the Russian Academy of Sciences, a building surrounded by a park. We were supposed to meet someone else, but since he was gone, the concierge scratched his balding head and decided he would take us to see Shamil.

He spoke candidly and convincingly. He didn't hesitate to criticise the government and discuss politically touchy subjects. He didn't ask about the details of our jobs, what we were doing in Daghestan or the purpose of our visit to the Daghestan Scientific Centre. Unlike 90 per cent of the people we met in Daghestan, he didn't immediately suspect us of being Polish—or even worse, NATO—spies. And finally, like any true highlander would, he invited us to his home. He stopped answering our emails about one year later. His silence lasted a good six months. Having followed recent events in Daghestan, we could only suspect that something bad had happened. The media were writing about the deaths of a few religious young men who had been active in journalism and academia; the first raids by Islamic militants, who would grow

in power within the coming years; and the first large-scale operations by special forces units.

No, he didn't go into the forest like some of his friends. He opted to emigrate. Like the nineteenth-century exiles who escaped the Russian-conquered
Caucasus and travelled to the Ottoman Empire, he became a modern-day
muhajir (immigrant). He chose Cairo, which gave him a chance to polish his
Arabic and broaden his knowledge of Islam. There's no room for people like
him in contemporary Daghestan. A young and ambitious person looking to
make something of his life can either become someone's client and accept the
pathological social and political system, or become a frustrated introvert, or a
militant.

Sure, he tried to find his place. He believed something could be done. His
enthusiasm, courage and ideas were an inspiration to others. He organised
conferences, lectures by interesting people and events designed to teach young
Daghestanis about the history of their own republic. Particularly the parts
that remain taboo in public debate: the anti-Bolshevik insurrections under the
banners of Islam, the deportation of the highlanders on to the plains and
Stalinist repression. Together with friends who shared his motivation, ideals
and deep Islamic faith, he led trips to the farthest corners of Daghestan, taking
pictures and shooting films during their hikes through the mountains. They
started publishing their own newspaper devoted to the history of Daghestan
and Islam. And they held incessant discussions. They believed they could
change the world, and that life in their republic could be better.

What they didn't realise at the time was that the fundamental rule of socio-
political systems like the one in Daghestan is 'don't step out of line'. Keep your
mouth shut and mind your own business. Don't try to change anything unless
you're prepared to take a beating. And when the beatings started, some of his
friends went into the woods and died the deaths of martyrs. Others, mostly
those with families, holed themselves up and abandoned any public activity.
Others abandoned their 'dangerous' views and 'suspicious' activities and went
into business or found a job with one of Daghestan's politicians-cum-warlords.
Shamil chose to move to the Middle East instead, and came back once things
began to cool down. But he didn't make his new home in Daghestan. They
still remembered all the times he had 'stepped out of line'. He chose Moscow,
a city he despised, but one that offered him much greater opportunities than
his home republic.

There are countless people like Shamil all over Daghestan. Since the early
nineties, the republic has been haemorrhaging a stream of young, intelligent

who can't find a place for themselves in the corrupt
ــd by post-communist apparatchiks and warlords. Some
ﻣ ve been punished for stepping out of line or were tipped off
ـﺎ it. Others see no future for themselves in a place where every-
ـ college diploma to a job in the public administration, police or
unﻲ ﻣ must be bought. They are disgusted by the language of media and
politicﻪ, which has changed little since the Brezhnev era, and by the complete
media blackout on the issues that really matter in the republic. Instead, politicians that had just recently been running local Komsomol branches or protection rackets were now repeating mantras that would make any thinking person
nauseous: clichéd slogans about the 'friendship of the nations of Daghestan',
the 'toil of the working masses of the republic' or the 'creative achievements of
the collectives'.

They pack their suitcases and go wherever their feet take them. As far away
as they can get from this solipsistic cesspool that has swallowed up more than
a few of their friends. Moscow, St Petersburg, Rostov-on-Don, Astrakhan:
these are the main destinations for Daghestan's young émigré intelligentsia.
More and more of them are choosing the Middle East, settling in countries
such as Saudi Arabia, Egypt, Jordan Syria and the United Arab Emirates,
where they often become radical supporters of the jihad and of the transformation of Daghestan into an Islamic state. They believe in neither democracy
nor dialogue with the West, and they accept no compromise. If Russian rule
over the Caucasus ever weakens and chaos creeps in, they may return to
Daghestan to impose their own order. The result may resemble Afghanistan
under the rule of the Taliban.

* * *

'There is a dangerous intellectualisation of radical Islam under way.' One of
Russia's best-known specialists on Islam doesn't hide his horror as we talk in
the monumental building of the Russian Academy of Science's Institute of
Anthropology and Ethnography. 'Look at this magazine. Half of the authors
are already *shahid*s.'

He held in his hands the sole issue of a magazine that Shamil and his friends
managed to publish despite obstacles created by the authorities, a publication
so bold, interesting and different from what is usually written about
Daghestan and in Daghestan that it can easily be read in one sitting.

'Wahhabism is beginning to attract its own ideologues. It's not just a cover
for Chechen militants and human traffickers anymore. There is a growing

number of intellectuals among the Wahhabis, and they're beginning to attract young people.'

Most Russian specialists on the Caucasus and Islam take a similar stance. They see the new Islam, represented by young, non-conforming intellectuals, as a deadly threat to Daghestan's secular political system and the territorial integrity of Russia.

Buried under stacks of books in their Moscow offices, they warn the government and society about 'dangerous Wahhabis' without stopping to consider the causes of the radicalisation of young Muslims in the Caucasus and without discerning between bearded thugs who kidnap people for ransom and, for instance, Bagauddin Kebedov, who calls for the reinstatement of 'the rule of Allah on earth'; between militants who plant bombs in 'saunas' and young intellectuals who can't and won't be a part of the status quo, many of whom, faced with government repression and harassment, choose to leave Daghestan or join the militants.

What if young intellectuals were given a chance? What if they were permitted to discuss their views openly, to print their papers and appear on television? What if they were included in public debate or even, with time, permitted to run for office? They would surely lay the foundations for a new Daghestani Muslim elite whose demands would include a return to tradition and the recognition of the important role of Islam in the life of the republic, but who would also be open to progress and diversity. Like the nineteenth-century Jadids, who wanted to reform Muslim society in tsarist Russia and adapt old models and solutions to new conditions without abandoning tradition. They turned to Islam and Sharia law for answers on how to build a socio-political system, but they wanted to reinterpret those sources to account for the changes that had taken place in the world over 1,000 years after the death of Muhammad.

But the authorities will never let them be heard. They're too afraid, as are the old post-communist elites. They panic at the sight of anyone who could undermine their position. Anyone who could prove there are viable alternative solutions. They prefer to scare people with the threat of 'Wahhabis' and 'terrorists'. One man to whom they showed too much tolerance managed to throw a wrench in their gears. The extraordinary and brave Nadirshakh Khachilayev, an idol to many young Daghestanis, called for the increased influence of Islam and Sharia law in the republic while also demanding radical political reform. Yet he did not want to achieve this through violent means, which he understood not all Daghestanis would support. Amid the political turbulence of the nineties, Khachilayev even managed to win a seat in the Russian Duma. But he stepped on too many toes, and was finally eliminated using an old, sure-fire method. He was torn to shreds by a bomb planted under his car.

* * *

Shamil invites us to dinner at a Moscow restaurant. 'You'll meet all kinds of people,' he says with an air of mystery. He was right. Following a group evening prayer, we sit down to eat. Fish soup, *plov* and to top it off, tea, sweets and fruit. No alcohol. Unhurried talks about religion, recent political events and family matters. Pensive, bearded faces, skullcaps and somewhat absent stares. Some of the men are dressed in Middle Eastern garb. The Moscow *jamaat*. Daghestanis, Tatars, Azeris, Ingushes, Afghans and Russian converts. New Muslims. The kind who only care if you believe in Allah. It doesn't matter to them what nationality you are, what language you speak or what colour your skin is. What's important is that you're a Muslim.

* * *

Most of those present at the dinner have followed a path similar to Shamil's. Religion had, until recently, been an entirely foreign concept to them; an antiquated tradition that deserved respect but was not to be taken seriously.

'I used to drink vodka like everyone else. I didn't pray or fast. I wasn't really a Muslim. And then something snapped in me when I attended graduate school in St Petersburg.'

'Non-stop partying and drinking in the dorms; drugs and easy girls; money and pleasure as the only goal in life. I realised that that wasn't what I wanted. That wasn't the world I wanted my children to grow up in.'

He set off to find his own path, his own views and his own lifestyle. He found it in Islam, the faith of his ancestors. He devoted himself to the study of the religion, reading the Qur'an, the hadith and treatises by famous Muslim philosophers, both classical and contemporary. He became interested in Islam as it was practised in the West and the life of Muslim communities in non-Muslim countries. He began attending the mosque, learned how to pray and gave up drinking. He made an effort to fulfil Allah's commandments.

In the eyes of his colleagues at university, he had become a madman. As an obstinate Daghestani highlander, he didn't particularly care. The real problems only started when, having completed his doctorate, he returned to Daghestan. Shamil's mother, father and siblings thought he had gone mad.

They feared their son had fallen in with religious extremists, or that he had been brainwashed by some cult. They were ashamed before their neighbours and relatives, especially at Shamil and Zarina's wedding, at which, upon the groom's request, no alcohol was served. Or at least it wasn't supposed to be served: his uncles managed to smuggle in a few bottles of moonshine, secretly serving it under the table.

* * *

Alongside Putin's Soviet Orthodox Russia, there is another, Islamic Russia. Not just in Daghestan, Chechnya and Tatarstan, but also in Moscow, St Petersburg and Nizhny Novgorod. A Russia that wears beards and bows down toward Mecca. A Russia that reads Russian-language Islamic websites and buys at shops that only sell halal products. A Russia that goes to Muslim medical centres and Muslim marriage agencies. Mosques in big Russian cities are crowded; sermons by famous Muslim teachers draw enormous crowds. And it is not at all rare for Russians to convert to Islam. Islam still occupies a tiny niche in Russia, a narrow margin of the Russian world. But it might one day become a real force on the Russian political scene.

CHECHNYA

15

THE MERCENARY

A woman occupying the bottom bunk in the Brest–Moscow train listens with interest as we talk about the Caucasus. She appears to understand Polish, and reacts enthusiastically whenever a Chechen place name comes up: Grozny, Gudermes, Vedeno.

'I'm Chechen. I've been living outside of Warsaw for six years,' Yakha says in quite fluent Polish. 'We fled Chechnya in 2003. My husband fought in the war, and they were looking for him. We were lucky enough to be given refugee status. Hardly anyone gets that anymore. Chechens arriving in Poland are often tossed into prison, just like that, for no reason.'

'Oh, Polish prisons aren't that bad. I did three months near Szczecin.' An amiable middle-aged man, clearly familiar with the topic, joins the conversation.

'Were you a refugee?' the woman asks.

'No—a smuggler,' he admits unreservedly. 'I could have paid a fine instead, but I was too ashamed to ask my family for the money. We had a pretty international cell. There was a Dutch guy, some drug addict from Germany, an Arab and a Moroccan. I must have put on 8 kilos! They caught us running vodka. I took things a bit too far with that job. I put 100 litres of pure grain alcohol in the trunk and I drove it clear across Poland. And I almost made it, but they caught me in Szczecin. Someone must have had a dry wedding that night! Back in the early nineties, a bribe of a few dollars would get you across the border with a whole trunk of vodka ... I've done it all ...' he says, pondering for a moment. 'And then I've served my country ...' He falls silent, as if considering whether it would be wise to say more. Could he be talking about *that* war?

'They say things have gone back to normal in Chechnya,' I offer, hoping to steer the conversation back to the topic.

'Things were peaceful for a while,' Yakha sighs. 'Now the terrorists are blowing themselves up again, taking innocent people with them. It used to be that they'd only target the army and the police.'

'What are you saying? Soldiers and policemen aren't people?' Vasiliy asks, irritated. 'I fought in Chechnya,' he adds, choosing his words carefully, as if fearful of starting an argument. 'I was a ...'

'Were you a *kontraktnik* or a conscripted soldier?' interrupts Yakha, somewhat upset.

'A *kontr* ...'

'You should be ashamed of yourself! How could you kill innocent people— children? And for money? You animal! Shooting people for money!' Yakha shouts.

'I was shot at too. It was your Dudayev who started the war.'

'He wasn't ours at all. They installed him just so he would start a war.'

'What do you mean he wasn't yours? You elected him—he's yours.'

'I don't know who voted for him, but it sure wasn't me.'

One would assume that Dzhokhar Dudayev, a symbol of the Chechen struggle for independence, would be considered a national hero by most Chechens. Warsaw named a roundabout after him, and he has his own street in Ukrainian Lviv. He is adored by Chechen émigré intellectuals, who think back on their homeland with nostalgia and dream of an independent republic. In their warm, safe apartments in the suburbs of Vienna, Paris and Oslo, they dream of liberating their country from Russian rule.

Many average Chechens have a somewhat different view of the early nineties, when Chechnya declared independence, followed three years later by the outbreak of the First Chechen War. For them, making ends meet was a greater priority than securing independence. The idea of national liberation, much less taking up arms for the cause, didn't even cross their minds. But when Russian forces rolled into Chechnya in 1994, they stood firmly behind Dudayev's militants. Memories were revived of the nineteenth-century Caucasian War, the uprisings against the tsar and Soviet rule and finally the deportation of Chechens to Central Asia, the most tragic page in their history. The determination of this tiny nation, combined with the internal crises of clay-footed Russia in the nineties, resulted in an unexpected outcome: in the autumn of 1996, after a daring recapture of Grozny from Russian hands, federal forces withdrew from Chechnya. The famous Khasavyurt Accord was signed, in which the Kremlin recognised the republic's autonomy and which Chechnya believed to be a peace treaty. For Russia, as it soon turned out, Khasavyurt Accord was merely a ceasefire, a temporary break from suppressing the rebellious highlanders who dared to stand up to the empire. Chechens were triumphant, while the world gasped in disbelief. But the celebration was not to last long. Ruined by war, recognised by no one except the Afghan Taliban, the republic descended into chaos. Chechnya in the latter half of the nineties was a landscape of clan warfare, organised crime and training camps for Islamic terrorists. Dreams of independence were dashed in 1999, when Prime Minister Vladimir Putin, inexplicably hailed a 'liberal' by Western analysts, sent forces back into Chechnya. The republic descended into chaos once more, and hundreds of thousands of people fled in panic, seeking refuge from indiscriminate Russian bombing. Several years of terror and ruthless raids, known as *zachistki*, took their toll on the people, who soon forgot about Dudayev and the hope of independence. Their only dream was that the shooting, the killing and the torture would stop. They were prepared to submit to any leader who would guarantee their safety and provide a roof over their heads. Chechnya had been subdued—at least for the time being.

* * *

'You bribed someone so you could become a *kontraktnik*, didn't you?' Yakha won't let go.

'I didn't bribe anyone.'

'You did it for the money.'

'What money? They paid me 3,500 roubles,[1] and another 3,500 for my wife, in case I didn't come back.'

'For the money ...'

'My sons were growing up. What was I supposed to do?'

'What do you think other people did? No one had a job. You should have opened your own market stall like everyone else.'

'Do I look like I know anything about business? The army was the only life I knew. I learned how to fight in Afghanistan. I didn't want my sons to be wanderers like me. I wanted to give them an education and a head start in life. That's a chance I didn't get. I come from a very poor family. Life in the USSR was modest, but you never had to worry about tomorrow. And then the trouble started. I saved up for a year so that my son could go to university. I thought I'd have enough for an apartment, but boy was I wrong! It was small change. At least he's studying in St Petersburg.'

'You don't even have your own apartment? Or a family home?' Yakha asks, not without a hint of sympathy.

'No, my parents live in a *kommunalka*,[2] and my wife and I are always on the move, renting rooms here and there.'

'Oh, that must be a tough life ...'

Yakha and Vasiliy are absorbed in conversation, as if forgetting about the war—a topic that should, it seems, create a chasm between them. They reminisced about the seventies: the years of their youth, the idealised decade of stability and the modest but long-awaited period of prosperity under Brezhnev; a time the middle generation looks back upon with fondness. Both of them now live the life of drifters, never knowing where they'll end up in a year or two. Yakha lives in Poland, and is thinking of moving to the West. She wants to go back to Chechnya, but she worries about what would happen to her husband. Her children go to school and have friends in Poland, and don't want to leave. Her husband, who is uncomfortable with taking such 'unmanly' work as cleaning or odd jobs, is unemployed. Like most Caucasian men, he would prefer to drive a taxi, work as a security guard or perhaps earn a living as a night watchman. Yakha travels back and forth between Poland and Chechnya, buying clothes in the former and selling them in the latter, and makes some money on the side as a cleaner. She and her husband rent a tiny studio apartment in the Warsaw suburb of Wołomin. Vasiliy has crossed thousands of kilometres in search of work, trying his luck in such far-flung destinations as the oil fields of the Russian north, Siberia and the aforementioned Polish city of Szczecin.

As we listen in on their conversation, it is hard to resist the impression that despite their first-hand experience of both wars, they have more in common than divides them. Both are, in a sense, victims of the new system, in which the poorest and least resourceful citizens, those unable to take advantage of the benefits of capitalism, have suffered the most. They describe their lives in ironic terms: 'survival [*vyzhivaniye*]'—living day to day with no certainty about what tomorrow will bring.

They share more than their hardship: they share a common past and vivid memories. All across the former Soviet Union, people separated by the conflicts that arose after the fall of the empire still look back on old times with nostalgia. Russians, Ukrainians and Belarusians aren't the only ones who share this sentiment. The average Georgian or Chechen may rant against

Russian imperialism, but will wax nostalgic when prompted with a question about Soviet times, fondly thinking back on his friends in Moscow and Leningrad, holidays in the Crimea, military service on the Kamchatka Peninsula, and blue-eyed Ludmila—the secret crush of every boy in class. 'A paradise lost' would be the most apt description of how the USSR is viewed by most of its former citizens. 'I was born in the Soviet Union, I was made in the USSR,' Russian vocalist Oleg Gazmanov nostalgically sings in one of his best-known songs. He recalls the past glory of the Soviet state, listing the accomplishments its inhabitants were most proud of: from Yuri Gagarin to the atom bomb and the country's victory in the Second World War. Gazmanov's song would be met with smiles of condescension in the West. We don't understand how anyone could have positive associations with the 'evil empire'. Yet the average Russian, Uzbek or Armenian will speak of the period with almost teary-eyed pride.

* * *

The train pulls out of Minsk around midnight. Just a few more stops—Orsha, Smolensk and Vyazma—and the locomotive will grind into the Belorussky terminal in Moscow. Most of the passengers have dozed off in their bunks. Vasiliy stares through the window ... I want to ask him more about war but I give up half way through. Why awake even more nightmares of the time ...

Kontraktnik ... In the Russian Caucasus, the word sounds nearly as ominous as 'Nazi' does in Poland. Dogs of war, mercenaries, savages, war criminals seething with hatred toward 'blacks'. Few enlisted out of patriotism. 'Reinstating constitutional order [*vostanovleniye konstitutionnogo poriadka*][3] 'and the 'struggle against international terrorism [*borba s miezhdunarodnym terrorizmom*]',[4] as the First and Second Chechen Wars were formally known, were of little concern to them. Nor did they go to war for glory or prestige. Public opinion was ambiguous with regard to the mercenaries who fought in Chechnya. The prevalent attitude was that of fear bordering on pity. While most Russians supported 'their boys' in the fight against the 'blacks', the soldiers weren't regarded as heroes, unlike veterans of the Great Patriotic War or the war in Afghanistan. The new generation of servicemen went to war because they saw no other place for themselves. Others did it for the money, having deluded themselves into believing that a tour of duty in Chechnya would let them and their families escape poverty and lead to a relatively comfortable life. Once they arrived at the front, the ones who weren't killed soon turned feral. Fed with stories of the 'terrorists' cruelty, and driven by a primordial fear for their own lives, they took the lives of others. Few ever went back to a normal life, but many came back to Chechnya, unable to fit in at home or even find a common language with their wives and children again. They could do nothing but shoot and conduct *zachistki*. The criminals themselves became the victims.

16

THE SHAHIDS

'Don't go there! You're going to get murdered! Or raped, if you're lucky. They'll throw you in a *zindan*,[1] torture you, pull out your nails, and scald you with boiling water. They'll be on your tail as soon as you arrive. People are scared. No one will take you in. Masked men will come in the middle of the night and tear up the apartment. They could plant drugs or weapons. It's never been this bad. Bomb attacks happen all the time, terrorists are blowing themselves up. Don't go. Not now. You're putting yourself and the people you meet in danger. You'll be lucky to come back alive.' This is merely an excerpt from the half-hour 'lecture' given to me by Dagman, a Chechen refugee in Poland, when she heard I was planning to go to Chechnya.

* * *

'Grozny, Gudermes, Samashki, Grozny!' calls a *marshrutka* driver in the Daghestani city of Khasavyurt. I'm sitting at the end of the van, making sure to remain inconspicuous. To avoid drawing attention, I've put on a black blouse, an ankle-length dress, a headscarf, high-heeled black shoes and my first communion jewellery.

I receive a text message from Poland: 'A *shahidka* blew herself up in downtown Grozny.' Reports of this type, which I find regularly in Russian online newspapers, cease to make an emotional impression on me. In the summer of 2009, attacks of all types were an almost daily occurrence, from bombs planted next to police stations, to bicycle-bombers sacrificing their lives to kill one or two policemen. 'It's just another attack,' I think to myself, but with

Grozny just an hour away, I find it hard to suppress the fear. I can't help but think about Dagman's admonition.

"'Should I go back?'" I begin to have second thoughts. "'But if she's already blown herself up, then today's mission is probably accomplished.'" "'Should I wait it out and come back when things calm down?'"

It probably wasn't the best time for a tour of the Caucasus. In the last three months alone, over 300 people had died in bomb explosions, raids and clashes in Daghestan, Chechnya and Ingushetia. Military and police reinforcements were brought into Daghestan. Pedestrians give a wide berth to the masked tactical anti-terrorist teams that have begun showing up on the streets. It isn't clear who they fear more: the terrorists or the very forces brought in to fight them. The avoidance of men in uniform is driven as much by pragmatism as it is by fear. They are, after all, the primary target of bomb attacks. *Marshrutka* drivers avoid the 'most popular' (i.e. most frequently attacked) police stations, while the mere sight of a policeman is enough to make people hastily cross the street. The officers themselves are no less afraid. They avoid forming groups and keep their weapons ready at all times. They quit as soon as other sources of income become available. The high risk and lack of prestige (or scorn drawn by the position) make it hard to recruit new officers. According to official sources, police began patrolling the streets in plain clothes after a series of attacks launched on police stations in early autumn 2009. The unofficial story is that officers began to procure (i.e. buy) doctors' notes en masse to avoid duty. Shootings can be heard every day. Police stations are entrenched in sandbags, behind which snipers lie ready to fend off surprise attacks.

"'They'll probably be searching the women more thoroughly today. But blondes? Russian soldiers seem only to search young brown-haired men.'" Ever since President Medvedev lifted the anti-terrorist regime in April 2009, foreigners can travel freely to Chechnya. So perhaps my attempts to blend in are unnecessary after all? But will the policemen believe that the purpose of my trip, as stated by my visa, is tourism? That I've come to Chechnya to visit mosques and fountains? And what about the camera, video camera and voice recorder in my backpack (or my shopping bag, as no one carries a backpack in these parts)?

The *marshrutka* stops at the border between Daghestan and Chechnya. A young soldier idly glances through the open door. I let out a sigh of relief as he lets us through without checking our passports.

* * *

The centre of the Chechen capital is heavily guarded by police. Automobile traffic has been shut down. A bomb exploded at the corner of Putin and Peace streets. While bombings, including suicide attacks, are no rare occurrence in Chechnya, there is a sense of agitation in the air.

Hussein, a lawyer acquaintance, meets us at the Minutka bus station and takes us home. His mother, who is busy in the kitchen, greets us warmly and automatically puts the kettle on for tea.

'I heard an explosion. I was in the area'—she starts after a while. 'Bystanders ran over to stare at the scene of the attack. I didn't go. I went home. What is there to see? I saw my share of corpses during the war. I grabbed my phone. Thank God my son wasn't in Grozny at that time. Will this ever end? I don't want to live like this,' she says. According to eyewitness accounts, 'the woman could barely walk, and seemed drunk or high. They made a zombie out of her. She was dressed in Muslim clothing.' Witnesses say she approached a police cruiser, attempting to open the door, when the bomb she was wearing detonated (or was detonated via cellphone). The car went up in flames. A *marshrutka* happened to be passing by at the exact moment of the explosion. Six passengers are said to be injured in the incident.

* * *

Hussein rests comfortably in an armchair. He looks very tired and sleepy.

'"I just got back from the morgue"'—Hussein suddenly joins into our conversation, which he didn't seem to have been listening to at all. '"There's nothing left of the *shahidka* but her head and toes. The body was ripped to shreds. She was wearing an approximate of 10 kilograms of TNT."'

Her identity remains unknown. Was she Chechen? Ingush? An inhabitant of Daghestan? We don't know who or what drove her to take her own life and the lives of others. Was it the promise of paradise that is said to await those martyred in the jihad against the infidels? Or, as some propose, could it have been money? Perhaps she sought revenge? The brutality of the security forces often pushed Chechens, among them many women, to commit suicide bombings, especially during the Second Chechen War. The torture, rape and humiliation they experienced in jail made revenge more important to them than saving their own lives.

* * *

One of the would-be terrorist martyrs was Bilal. Ordered by his commanders to leave Chechnya and wait for the signal, he arrived in Poland in 2002 and ended up in a refugee centre. Curious of the world around him, he began to make trips around the area. He read books borrowed from the public library, and started meeting people. He made a few friends in Poland and decided to learn the language. A few months after his arrival, he received an email with his orders. He was to get behind the wheel of a TNT-packed truck and ram it into a building chosen by his superiors. His commanders had already bought him a ticket to Moscow. He went to say goodbye to his friends, tears welling in his eyes. A librarian, whom he had befriended during his stay in Poland, tried to persuade him not to go. What difference did it make where he died? He had given his word, and that they would track him down and kill him if he backed out. He called his father, asking if he could 'chicken out'. The librarian and her family chipped in to pay for a ticket and for him to be smuggled across the border. He made it, and managed to reach Vienna. His friend obediently boarded the train from Warsaw to Moscow ...

Bilal wrote an email to my friend after settling down in Vienna. He wrote that everything is fine and that he hates 'all that dammed war, all that stupid struggle for no one knows what'.

* * *

The world first learned of Chechen terrorism in 1991. Not even the Chechens had ever heard of the young radical Shamil Basayev before he hijacked a plane from the North Caucasian city of Mineralnye Vody to Istanbul in an attempt to draw attention to the events in Chechnya. The republic, unnoticed by the international community, was in the process of declaring its independence, taking advantage of the confusion brought about by the collapse of the Soviet Union. Basayev achieved his goal. It may have been the first time in history that Chechnya made international headlines. A few years later, the world watched as Chechen militants attacked two hospitals in southern Russia, taking thousands of hostages in a reckless attempt to win glory and change the course of the first war with Russia, which the Chechen rebels had been losing. Their leader, again, was Shamil Basayev. In June 1995, he led a team of a few dozen militants in storming a hospital in Budyonnovsk, demanding that the Kremlin pull its forces out of Chechnya and commence peace talks with Dudayev. The Russian government backed down, agreeing to negotiate and let Basayev return to Chechnya unhindered, where he was greeted as a national hero. The Russians, however, reneged on the agreement within a matter of days, and attacks resumed with even greater force. A few months later, Salman Raduyev set off in the footsteps of Basayev, apparently hoping to rival Shamil's glory and earn a reputation as a fearless and ruthless *dzhigit*. Hospital patients taken hostage by Raduyev's forces in the Daghestani town of Kizlyar greeted him as a hero. At the time, Daghestanis were rooting for the Chechens, and many volunteered to serve as human shields when the militants decided to retreat into Chechnya after negotiations failed. The Russians surrounded them near the village of Pervomayskoye, but the militants broke through the block-ade. Despite his tactical failure, Raduyev succeeded in achieving his selfish goal: he had become the second most notorious Chechen terrorist.

That's it, as far as terrorism in the First Chechen War goes. There were no suicide or airliner bombings. Basayev and Raduyev may have employed terror-ist methods, but to call them Islamic terrorists would be a gross overstatement. Like a significant majority of Chechen militants at the time, their motivation lay not in religion, but in their nationalist views and their desire to play a role in the Chechen struggle for independence. Their green headbands were noth-ing more than decoration.

Religiously motivated terrorism was a product of the Second Chechen War. Contrary to expectations, the first 'Islamic terrorists' were not responsible for the most infamous terrorist attacks in Russian history, the September 1999 incidents in Moscow, Volgodonsk and Buynaksk, the aftermath of which lofted Vladimir Putin into power. One could hardly consider his friends at the FSB, who in all probability orchestrated the attacks, to be 'Islamic terrorists'. The first *shahids* were women. Khava Barayeva—the sister of one of the most brutal Chechen commanders Arbi Barayev, who was guilty of ransom kidnap-pings—was the first female martyr to get behind the wheel of a truck and attack a Russian military base in 2000. Then there was Aiza Gazuyeva, a teacher from Urus-Martan, who strapped on a vest of TNT a year later and 'embraced' General Gadzhiyev, the despised local tyrant who was responsible for the death of her husband and two brothers, and the beating of her father.

That's when it started in earnest. Terrorist attacks conducted by martyrs, known as *shahids*, peaked in 2002–4. The series of gruesome incidents began at Moscow's Dubrovka theatre and culminated in the storming of a school in the North Ossetian town of Beslan. Terrorists were usually recruited from among youths who had suffered harm at the hands of Russian soldiers and were willing to die, torn to shreds along with their victims, in the name of revenge. They were trained in camps run by Basayev in the mountainous region of Chechnya, after which they were sent off to an invisible front. They would blow themselves up on buses, trains, planes and in the Moscow metro. They would drive trucks stacked with explosives into government and military buildings. One *shahidka* went as far as to slip into a rock concert in Moscow, perpetrating a massacre of innocent youths. That's when the world learned about Chechen terrorism. Russia was shocked by the incident at the Dubrovka theatre and, later, the tragic events in Beslan in 2004, where Russian forces stormed a school in which Chechen rebels had been holding children hostage, hundreds of whom perished in the aftermath.

The first stage of the escalation of Islamic terrorism in Russia ended with the Beslan school hostage crisis. Perhaps the militants (if such a term may even be used to describe men who had killed children) decided that terrorism was ineffective, and that risking such high losses did not produce the desired results. After all, the Russian government was completely unwilling to compromise, even when it came to the lives of children. According to another, more conspiratorial, theory, the attacks ended when they ceased to be of any more use to politicians in Moscow. Those who sought to exploit the public's fear of further violence had succeeded in expanding their power while limiting democracy and personal liberties in Russia, all in the name of the war on terror.

* * *

It is the summer of 2009. After nearly four years of relative peace in Chechnya, the *shahid*s have returned, and they are clearly more than just a handful of desperate and isolated radicals seeking revenge. The regularity, frequency and precision of the attacks all point to the existence of a professional mastermind. According to Chechen President Ramzan Kadyrov, whose reputation and political position is the most harmed by the attacks, the *shahid*s are being trained by international terrorists from Arab nations, with financial support from 'hostile Western states', particularly the United States. American complicity in the terrorist attacks in the Northern Caucasus is allegedly proved by the fact that the United States trained and supported Osama bin Laden during the Soviet war in Afghanistan. To prove their assertions, the Chechen government released footage of Kadyrov personally interrogating four would-be bombers who were planning to blow themselves up in Shali, a small Chechen town located in the Caucasian foothills. After berating the young boys with a litany of insults, Kadyrov begins to threaten them.

'Don't you know that Chechens practise blood feuds? Don't you know what kind of trouble you'd bring down on your family, your father, and your mother, even in ten or twenty years?'

Kadyrov was not one to make idle threats, and had his bearded henchmen pay repeated 'visits' to the militants' brothers and families. Those for whom these encounters ended with a few missing teeth or their houses going up in flames could consider themselves fortunate. Ramzan was not the only one to resort to collective responsibility. A few years ago, Russian Prosecutor General Vladimir Ustinov proposed in parliament that the army take the families of mujahideen hostage, and hold them until the militants have a change of heart and decide to turn themselves in.

Under obvious duress, the would-be *shahids* admitted in front of cameras to having been recruited into the ranks of Arab militants, who gave them money and taught them how to use the TNT-packed '*shahid* belts'. Kadyrov picked up one such belt and, holding it up to one of the boys, asked him:

'So you wanted to go to heaven? May you be damned! Don't you know that suicide is considered a grave sin in Islam? It would be different if you blew yourself up to kill an Arab devil. Then you would be sure to go to heaven.'

We don't know who they were or if they're still alive. Did they actually have connections to the Islamic militant underground, or was the footage, as some suggest, fabricated for propaganda purposes, just as it is when boys are snatched off the streets of Makhachkala, murdered, dressed up as scary mujahideen, complete with Kalashnikov rifles, and shown on TV? Local authorities and security forces use such methods to convince the public and the Kremlin that they are, in fact, fighting dangerous terrorists.

Although the ties between the Caucasian underground and international Islamic terrorist networks do exist, and a considerable numer of local militants pledge allegiance to the Islamic State, they are, so far, of little local consequence. With the conflicts raging in Syria, Iraq or Afghanistan, what interest do the ideologists behind the international jihad have in a few *shahids* plotting to blow themselves up in some forsaken Caucasian town? Islamic State and Al Qaida have other issues on their minds. For them the North Caucasus serves barely as a good source of experienced fighters. Bombings in Chechnya, Daghestan or Kabardino-Balkaria (which happen less frequently since many local militants left for the Middle East) are usually orchestrated by local ideologists and commanders, Caucasian tough-guys who look down at the 'delicate' and 'clamorous' Arabs. All they want from them is money. Islamic State seems to be generous when it comes to recruitment of the new fighters but funding for the Caucasian Emirate is hard to secure. How do they still find volunteers prepared to give their lives for the utopian vision of an Islamic state in the Caucasus?

'They have their ways ...' says a young man from a stall at the Khasavyurt bazaar. 'They seek out the weak and lost; not men of strong character, with leadership qualities or a knack for business, but mama's boys and losers.' He explains that men who are ridiculed and scorned, who can only dream of starting their own families, are easily manipulated and deluded with praise and the promise of eternal happiness after their 'heroic' deaths. 'They tried this with my neighbour ...' he adds. 'Some guys wouldn't understand, what is happening ...' he continues after a while. 'Some of them are given bags or packages, which they are told to take to specific locations. The bombs are detonated via cellphone by their commanders.'

'Are there any driven by ideals?' I ask.

'Yes, there are some. They consider Shamil Basayev a hero and an idol. They listen to stories told by friends and read the propaganda posted on militant websites, dreaming of joining the jihad and dying a martyr's death. They are proud to have been chosen. But, you know, many just want revenge. For the death of their loved ones or their own humiliation, which they can bear no longer.' I don't ask for details, places or stories. This is not the knowledge to share. This is not 'safe' knowledge. He thanks me for respecting that and goes back to his work.

* * *

The wave of attacks that occurred in 2009 suggested that the mujahideen have gone back to the tactics employed in previous years, making terrorism their primary method of the struggle. But can we be certain? Is it merely a coincidence that the wave of suicide bombings occurred right after the anti-terrorist regime was lifted in Chechnya, against the request of the Russian security forces? While this may sound like a conspiracy theory, it cannot be ruled out that the military has been turning a blind eye to terrorist attacks in order to achieve its own goal, namely, to sustain a constant sense of impending threat in the Caucasus. An unstable Caucasus translates into increased spending on the military and police, and a greater influence of these structures on the country. It enables the pursuit of careers and illegal business opportunities. Every army in the world, when left to its own devices, seeks opportunities for self-fulfilment—its own private wars that will enable it to grow more powerful. The Russian army is no exception, especially considering Russia has more or less remained in a constant state of war for hundreds of years. The greatest tragedy, however, is that—if the above is true—Russian generals have chosen to take the path of least resistance, pursuing self-fulfilment in their own country and waging wars against their fellow citizens.

* * *

The image of the head of the *shahidka* is passed around Grozny that night—in a text message.

17

RAMZAN'S CITY

Downtown Grozny is closed off again today. We have no hope of getting across town. All around us are bearded Kadyrovites and the widely feared special police forces.

'Someone must have blown himself up again,' comments Zaur, my Chechen friend in his fifties. 'No, wait: it's Friday, isn't it? Then it's probably "our guy" attending Friday prayers. He's a bit late,' he says sarcastically, glancing at his watch.

When Ramzan comes to pray, the entire grounds of the Akhmad Kadyrov Mosque are sealed off to everyone but him and his bodyguards. Automobile traffic is shut down within a 1 kilometre radius, bringing the entire city centre to a standstill.

'There used to be a statue of Akhmad Kadyrov under 24-hour guard, but they took it down last week'—Zaur points to an empty square as we walk around the area. 'Kadyrov Jr finally figured out that the statue was a violation of Islamic norms,' Zaur laughs. Or maybe Ramzan wanted to get rid of the last symbolic trace of his predecessor, Alu Alkhanov, who put the statue up and whom the current president unceremoniously expelled from the republic upon taking office? That's another possible explanation.

'What about billboards?'

'Billboards he likes too much to tear them down just because of Islam. Don't you like his "golden thoughts?"' Zaur jokes sarcastically. 'He can't even express them in proper Russian. But we are like Turkmens now, we love "our man". We have to—if we don't want to end up in his Tsentoroy prison.'

* * *

Is Ramzan Kadyrov the face and symbol of contemporary Chechnya? Capable of protecting the republic's interests? Primitive and cruel, would this dictator sell his soul to the devil for power and money? Is he an unfaithful, Moscow-serving 'dog', a traitor to the Chechen nation and to Muslims?

For educated people like Zaur, Ramzan Kadyrov is a simple country boy, who, like the entire generation of young Chechens, grew up in the First Russian–Chechen War, in which he fought on the side of the militants. A boy who, if not for the circumstances of war, would have had no chance of rising higher than the rank of a traffic patrolman, and certainly would not have become president.

Ramzan Kadyrov's path to power was paved by his father, a cunning actor who managed to maintain his position in the Chechen political elite despite drastically changing circumstances. Akhmad Kadyrov was a supporter of the pro-independence camp in the nineties. As a mufti of Chechnya, he called on its citizens to wage jihad against Russia. But when the republic—left to itself by Moscow—descended into chaos in 1996–9, he began to distance himself from the Chechen leadership, criticising President Aslan Maskhadov for his perceived tolerance of Islamic radicals. Kadyrov finally broke off ties with the pro-independence camp when Russian forces marched back into Chechnya in 1999. He opted to collaborate with the Russians, and in the process became a traitor in the eyes of most Chechens. In exchange for his loyalty, the Kremlin appointed him head of the republic's civil administration, and later, in 2003, president of Chechnya.

His term did not last long. Kadyrov was killed in an attack in Grozny in 2004, half a year after taking office. A bomb placed under the VIP stands exploded on 9 May during a parade commemorating the end of the Second World War. According to the official version, Islamist militants were behind the plot, while the unofficial version of the story points to Russian generals who had grown dissatisfied with Kadyrov's growing influence and Putin's preferential treatment of the Chechen president.

With no experience in politics, the twenty-seven-year-old Ramzan took over after his father, first as a deputy minister, then prime minister, officially becoming president only in 2007. The initial reaction to his leadership was of amusement, particularly after his first television appearance, just hours after his father's death, which showed him arriving at the Kremlin dressed in a blue track suit. But the new Chechen leader quickly showed the public what he was capable of, using all means at his disposal to silence critics, forcing them into exile, locking them up in illegal prisons, one of them located in his hometown of Khosi-Yurt (Tsentoroy), or simply murdering them. His thugs ventured as far as Moscow and Vienna to chase down enemies who had dared get on their boss's bad side.

* * *

New buildings of better or worse quality are springing up throughout the Chechen capital. New government offices, apartments blocks, modern high-rises. And while the average citizen of the republic will never be able to afford a flat in one of the modern high-rises, they may take some consolation in the fact that if Moscow companies are investing in Grozny, then chances are slim that war will return to the republic anytime soon.

'They're going to collapse soon,' says Zaur. 'They were erected in a slipshod manner, using the cheapest construction material available. You know—if Moscow gives money for marble, they build with plastic. Guess where the money goes. This country is heading towards collapse,' Zaur says pessimistically. Like many open-minded and educated people of his generation he cannot accept the Ramzan regime and dreams of its imminent collapse.

'Only the façades of the buildings were painted during the preparations for a visit by the street's patron,' continues Zaur, pointing at Putin's boulevard. Grozny's main boulevard has born several names over the years—from Lenin (a stock toponym used from Kaliningrad to Vladivostok), to Imam Shamil and Dudayev. In this century alone, it has been renamed after two heroes of the republic: the aforementioned Kadyrov senior, whose stretch of the street ends at the mosque, and Vladimir Putin, whose name was given to several blocks of a tree-lined drag with crescent moon-adorned streetlights in a renovated part of town. Is this a symbol of the power-sharing arrangement between Moscow and the Kadyrov regime?

Ramzan's relationship with Moscow is almost as close as his embrace with Putin, as depicted on the billboards. Rather than make demands for independence, the president emphasises the republic's place in the Russian Federation. Does that make him a Russian patriot? Only formally. In practice, Ramzan Kadyrov has achieved a great degree of independence from Moscow and employs a number of methods to reduce Russian influence in the republic. The one form of Russian intervention he does welcome is that of federal funding, for which he lobbies heavily. Like his father, Ramzan seeks actual, rather than formal autonomy, particularly with regard to the economy, a goal in which he has achieved partial success. Kadyrov's future objective will be to take control of Chechnya's oil deposits, which currently remain outside his reach and establish closer international relations, especially with the Middle East. One of the first achievements of Ramzan as a Chechen leader was an official end of Russia's counterterrorist operation in Chechnya (in April 2009), which limited the republican government's power and posed an obstacle to communication with other countries. The granting of international status to the Grozny airport was one of the consequences of the lifting of the counterterrorist stigma. The first flight took off in November 2009, setting course for Saudi Arabia. In the subsequent years Ramzan enjoyed even more independence and impunity. His private army grew stronger, while the influence of the federal armed forces became limited. Chechnya enjoys now a greater autonomy than during Dudayev's rule in the nineties. Does it all mean that Kadyrov may lead a new Chechen independence movement in future? It seems highly unlikely. There is too much too lose.

* * *

'You've expected ruins, haven't you?' asks Zaur. 'No, they are smart, they put them all behind fences,' says Zaur as we head towards the suburbs. All relics of the unpleasant past seem to have been torn down in the city centre, but the authorities haven't been nearly as meticulous when it comes to the city's outskirts. In the suburbs, many people continue to live in ruined houses and hastily constructed barracks which overflow with refugees returning, more or less voluntarily, from camps in Ingushetia.

We approach a four-story half-renovated apartment complex. 'Are you alone, mother?' Zaur calls across the threshold of the door to one of apartments, before letting us in. 'I have guests. I'll explain later.' 'You can't trust people anymore. And you know, now we better not talk about him and those things at home, right?' asks Zaur in a convoluted manner without using his name. 'Walls have ears, you know.'

We enter the small apartment. Zaur's family is among the lucky few whose homes were not completely razed in the war. They have a place to live but they continue to set out buckets to collect rainwater from the leaking roof. After every strong gust of wind, they have to replace the foil screens in some of the windows.

* * *

Many of my Chechen friends from Grozny share Zaur's pessimistic view of Chechnya and Ramzan. There's no place for them in Chechnya where armed thugs roam the republic's newly built roads in their black Hummers and enjoy greater respect than intellectuals with extensive knowledge of literature and foreign languages who can do nothing to stop the violence penetrating their homeland. They can but mock Ramzan, if only quietly and with people they trust. Zaur and his mother have been in Grozny during the two wars. Nowadays they want to leave Chechnya at the first possibility. 'It was more scary during the war, but you felt part of the society. Now I don't, not anymore,' he concludes sadly.

* * *

Zaur emigrated a year later.

18

THE PILGRIMAGE

'My name is Ibragim. This is my passport,' says the man in *papakha*. 'These are the times we live in. You can't trust anybody.' It doesn't occur to me that the proper response would be to show my own papers. We get into the Volga.

'Remember: from now on, you're my relatives from Daghestan. Your father is the son of my paternal uncle's maternal cousin. That's how I'm going to introduce you to my friends,' says Ibragim. 'You're not really dressed right for a pilgrimage. You have to cover up all your private parts. We'll think of something.' A moment later a woman runs up to the car and hands us warm, black knee-high socks that are sure to cover up our ankles. The problem of our private parts has been solved.

'You're familiar with our customs, aren't you? Just follow my lead.'

We pick up two older men in the village of Chechen-Aul, from which the name of the republic is said to be derived. Ibragim introduces us in Chechen. We nod politely, smiling nervously. God forbid we shake hands or extend longer greetings. That would not befit a Caucasian woman.

Our knowledge of local customs is soon put to its first test. We pass a cemetery. The driver turns the music down. The passengers lift their hands to chest level. They pray in hushed voices and then draw their hands across their faces. We make awkward attempts to mimic their gestures. Our driver soon saves us from long conversations with the other passengers, who appear to be fooled by our disguises. He cranks up a Chechen *dhikr*—a collectively sung prayer that is the most important ritual practised by the most popular Sufi brotherhood in Chechnya, the Qadiriya. The rhythmic *la ilaha illallah*, supported by the resonant voices of the older men, accompanies us on our drive through the Chechen countryside.

We drive south-east, in the direction of forested mountains looming on the horizon. Business is booming for gate salesmen along the road. Most homes took heavy damage from gunfire. Maroon, green and black gates 2 to 3 metres tall hide signs of the war. Construction is under way in every village we pass; the republic is slowly lifting itself out of nearly two decades of collapse. The most persistent Chechens, those who managed to break through the red tape, were paid war retributions (albeit often reduced by half due to the 'commissions' for the officials along the way). Help comes from families abroad as well as relatives in Moscow or in the oil fields of the North, where many Chechens have found jobs. It's also possible to make a living in Chechnya itself, and not just in Ramzan's forces. Modest wages can be earned in hospitals and schools. Construction workers, repairmen and foremen are in demand. Like neighbouring Daghestan, Chechnya has been drawing a steady stream of Vietnamese immigrants, who have carved out a niche in trade and construction. The condition of the economy and the job market in the Caucasian republics could be much worse.

We pass towns and villages whose names we recognise from the media coverage of combat operations and *zachistki* that took place here just a few years before: Belgatoy, Shali, Serzhen'-Yurt. Military bases appear every few kilometres, usually on hilltops, surrounded by barbed wire. Could the end of counterterrorism operations, announced in April 2009 and widely covered by the Russian media, have been a lie? It appears that federal army bases in Chechnya have not shut down after all, and that part of the Russian forces remain in the republic. The soldiers that did stay behind spend most of their time in the barracks, preferring not to interfere in Chechen infighting.

We slow down as we approach a checkpoint reinforced with sandbags. Our driver puts his *papakha* on to appear more respectable. Despite being only fifty years old, Ibragim's grey beard and *papakha* let him easily pass for a distinguished elder, especially in the eyes of young Russian troops. Heavily armed and protected by bullet-proof vests, the soldiers eye the passengers but, to our relief, do not ask for our papers. It's clear that a car with three grandfathers in *papakha* and two country girls doesn't raise any eyebrows here.

'Heil Hitler!' the passengers mutter at the *kontraktniki* as we pull away from the checkpoint. Mercenaries are said to earn good money for serving in Chechnya. They're in no hurry to pull out, and neither are their commanders, who see it as an opportunity to prove themselves in the 'fight against terrorism'.

I can't shake the feeling that the man sitting next to me has figured out that Ibragim isn't telling the truth about us. But Aslan doesn't press the subject. That's how things are here. If a friend doesn't want you to know something, he must have his reasons. It comes as no surprise in post-war Chechnya: no one takes insult at such secrecy. As Chechens sometimes say, 'Too much truth is even worse.' You never know what bit of information might cause someone harm. Only one's closest friends and relatives can be trusted. Such an attitude is a result of living in constant fear and in the conviction that, at any moment, you may die or be abducted, interrogated or thrown into prison. Few have ever made it out. Some are said to have been tortured by Kadyrov himself. Why put yourself and your family in danger? Why tempt fate? Aside from the republic's relative stability and progressing economic recovery, mutual distrust and a climate of fear are two looming consequences of the Kadyrov regime, which deals ruthlessly with dissidents. People don't talk much about politics, especially in company. When asked privately, many Chechens admit they don't support the president's policies. But they won't criticise him openly either. 'What can I do? I live here,' we often hear.

Noticing my interest in the area and in the armoured personnel carriers that keep passing us, Aslan strikes up a conversation. 'This used to be a camp-ground for the Young Pioneers,' he explains, pointing out wooded hills by the village of Avtury. 'And over there you have hot springs. People used to come here from all over Russia. Even Gagarin once paid a visit.'

I stop myself before asking more questions. Too much interest in the war by a woman from the mountains of Daghestan would leave Aslan with no illusions as to my true identity. I continue to play along. So does Aslan. He starts a discussion that he probably would not engage in with a Daghestani woman, on the assumption that she wouldn't know what he was talking about (although this is not always true, it is generally believed in the Caucasus that women are not interested in politics and know nothing about it; and therefore, discussions on the topic are deemed pointless).

'A few years later Khattab set up his own camp here. He trained militants from all over the Caucasus and from Arab countries,' says Ibragim. Khattab has certainly left his mark in the history of Chechnya. He was born in Saudi Arabia, but his ancestors came from the Caucasus. If he were ever to write a résumé, he would have to list his profession as 'international terrorist with extensive experience'.

He began his career as a sixteen-year-old boy in Soviet-occupied Afghanistan. Then came Tajikistan and Bosnia, and, in the mid-nineties,

Chechnya. His poor grasp of Russian didn't keep him from becoming one of the most influential warlords in Chechnya. He formed his own militant unit, which earned a reputation for its bravery, during the First Chechen War. When combat died down, he began training militants ready to fight for the cause of an Islamic state in the Caucasus.

He made his base in the heavily wooded Vedensky District in the heart of Ichkeria, the historic land that gave its name to Dudayev's Chechen Republic of Ichkeria. Between the wars, Khattab settled down in the Caucasus for good, marrying a Daghestani woman and becoming good friends with Shamil Basayev. When fighting erupted again, he became Basayev's right-hand man and liaison to other terrorist organisations around the world. It was through him that the militants received financial support from Arab countries.

Russian security services repeatedly made false announcements of his death. It wasn't until the spring of 2002 that they finally succeeded, although Khattab did not die in battle, as would befit a mujahid. He was poisoned by a letter delivered by a militant who had been turned by the FSB. None of the few Arab volunteers ever achieved comparable fame and influence in Chechnya after Khattab's death. His training camps outside Serzhen'-Yurt and by the picturesque mountain lake Kazenoy-Am have once again grown over with grass. Perhaps they await the return of the Pioneers?

* * *

We arrive in the Vedensky District. Reconstruction has progressed slower here than on the plains surrounding Grozny. Many houses lie in ruin, and few of the bullet-riddled gates have been replaced. There are hardly any people to be seen on the streets. It seems that many of the inhabitants never returned to their homes. 'Caution Mines!' reads the red-and-white tape that has been used to fence off a 300-metre field, which remains uncleared despite the enormous financial support that has been pouring into Chechnya. Perhaps the army feels it might still be useful to have mined land in the mountain districts?

It suddenly dawns on me that I have not seen a single checkpoint or even as much as a soldier or police officer for quite a while. It appears the police only patrol the main roads. There have also been rumours of an informal agreement between the authorities and the militants, who continue to control some mountain areas, including the Vedensky District. The presence of local police and administration is only formal—they check their work off on paper and collect a salary. In reality, they have no say in any matters, and, in some extreme cases, do not even live in the villages they have been appointed to. Could it be that the district's inhabitants have remained faithful to their compatriot Shamil Basayev, who was born in the nearby village of Dyshne-Vedeno?

We park in front of an impressive complex of coloured marble buildings on Ertan-Korta, a hill near Tsa-Vedeno. The enormous stairs and ramps on either side lead to a small tomb at the top of the hill. Inside lies the grave of Kheda, mother of the Sufi master Kunta-haji, one of the most important figures in the Chechen pantheon of national heroes.

In the mid-nineteenth century, as the Caucasian War raged on and Imam Shamil led his soldiers into battle, Kunta-haji realised how great the casualties of war would be, and he called for Chechens to stand down and surrender their weapons. 'Your weapons shall not be rifles nor the *kindjal*,[1] but your prayer beads! Shun anything that resembles war, as long as the enemy does not come for your faith or dignity. Your strength lies in reason, patience, and justice,' he taught.

The despotic Shamil was displeased with Kunta-haji's pacifism and banished the sheikh from the Caucasus. He travelled to the Ottoman Empire and lived in Mecca for a while. He resumed his activities after the end of the Caucasian War. Although he did not change his views, his popularity among Chechens was treated with suspicion by the tsarist authorities, who saw his followers as a threat. He was arrested and sent to the distant city of Kaluga. In protest, several thousand of his supporters gathered in the town of Shali and marched, unarmed, toward the waiting army to demand the release of their teacher. Many believe that Kunta-haji would prevent the soldiers' weapons from firing. They fired. Four hundred people died. From then on, the brotherhood continued its work in secret, which did not prevent its ranks from growing. The followers of Kunta-haji—known around the world for their performance of an ecstatic *dhikr*, a ritual that involves running in a circle to the accompaniment of loud singing—believed that their sheikh did not die in exile, but lived on and would return as the Mahdi, or messiah, who would come down to earth to liberate the Chechens from Russian captivity and humanity from the devil's captivity.

Despite Soviet repression and the lack of a leader, the brotherhood was not dissolved. Kunta-haji's followers gathered in small groups in nearly every *aul*. In Kazakhstan, where Chechens were exiled in 1944, the Kunta-haji brotherhood became their only salvation and the social cement that kept them from losing heart and assimilating with the more populous nations (like Germans, Poles, Ukrainians, Russians[2] and others) who had also been thrown by fate on to the Kazakh steppe. Kunta-haji's followers splintered into a number of factions whose leaders preached the coming of justice and foretold the return of the Chechens to their homeland. Many of them promoted polygamy, a practice that had remained rare in Chechnya, justifying it on the grounds that it was the nation's only hope of survival after the death of thousands of men in exile and the fronts of the Second World War. The Chechens survived, and the Khrushchev Thaw enabled them to return to the Caucasus.

The stabilisation and relative prosperity of the sixties and seventies dealt a slight blow to the brotherhoods, but the collapse of the Soviet Union and Chechnya's declaration of independence marked their resurgence. This time, however, the followers of Kunta-haji abandoned their pacifist beliefs. They became the driving force behind the Chechen national independence movement, and thanks to foreign journalists, their *dhikr* was seen around the world, turning—against the intentions of the brotherhood—into a 'Chechen war dance', one of the 'trademarks' of Chechen separatism.

The wheel of history began to turn again, however, when the Kadyrovs, themselves active members of the brotherhood, came to power in Chechnya. The followers of Kunta-haji became the main force opposing the militants, among whom anti-Sufi fundamentalist views were gaining traction. By taking the side of Akhmad Kadyrov and, later, his son Ramzan, both active opponents of the 'Wahhabis', the brotherhood inevitably lent legitimacy to the regime. Formally, they became allies of Russian rule in Chechnya. It remains to be seen for how long.

* * *

We circle the tomb slowly, in silence, touching the walls that encircle Kheda's grave. People come here for different reasons: to pray, to venerate Kunta-haji and his mother or to ask the dead for help or the healing of a loved one. They believe that by visiting the *ziyarat*, or shrine, they receive *barakah*, or a blessing. These practices, while deeply rooted in the culture of the north-eastern Caucasus, in fact have little to do with Islam, which strictly forbids the veneration of anyone beside Allah. For this reason, they are strongly opposed by fundamentalists, who consider them manifestations of paganism and polytheism. 'Wahhabis' associated with Khattab even attempted to bomb the tomb in 1995, sparking outrage throughout Chechnya. It was as if someone had attempted to bomb Notre Dame Cathedral, claiming that the veneration of Mary had little to do with early Christianity. Anyone who would dare commit such an act would likely find himself in even greater trouble than Khattab's men.

Peering through a small window, we make out handwoven rugs arranged around a grave. Next to it lie shreds of a cloak and some items that likely belonged to Kheda. There is no time to get a good look. Facing the tomb, we walk backwards to the gate.

Before the war, this location housed a small but well-known *ziyarat*. Today it has grown into a pilgrimage centre capable of accommodating thousands of visitors from all over the Caucasus. Mosques have been erected, along with leisure facilities and space, in which the *dhikr* may be conducted. Nearby is a sacred spring from which pilgrims draw water, and which is believed to have healing properties.

The renovation and modernisation of *ziyarat*s across Chechnya was begun under orders from Akhmad Kadyrov. His policies were continued by Ramzan, who won the support of many members of the popular Qadiriya brotherhood, to which a number of his relatives belonged. Islam in its 'Sufi' or 'traditional' form was recognised as a native Chechen faith and was elevated to the level of national ideology, while Kunta-haji became Chechnya's number one hero, perhaps even outranking Imam Shamil himself. Once kept hidden from public view, the brotherhood's religious practices were used as a standard for the republic. The *dhikr*, once performed only in the brotherhood's small and relatively closed circles, was transformed into a public spectacle broadcast on Chechen television. Local media devote more and more air time to broadcasts of pilgrimages to *ziyarat*s, opening ceremonies at new mosques, animal sacrifices and public prayers offered for members of the Kadyrov family (for instance Ramzan's ten-year-old nephew, who crashed a car given to him by the president).

Kunta-haji's *dhikr* has even won the acceptance of the Russian authorities, who have nothing against its performance not only in Chechnya but even in Moscow. Each Thursday at dusk, just a few hundred metres from the busy Novokuznetskaya metro station, bearded men in knee-length tunics gather at a mosque known as the 'Tatar Mosque'. The police leave them alone. According to the latest Kremlin policies, these men are now considered 'our Chechens'.

* * *

Ibragim takes us to his home in Novye Atagi. 'Make yourselves at home. I'm off to the *dhikr*.' Ibragim changes into a loose, grey outfit commonly worn by members of the brotherhood and Sufi sheikhs, and dons a black *tubeteika*. He has recently assumed the function of *turkh*, or elder of the brotherhood. He is responsible for holding regular *dhikr*s and prayers in his village, and he also organises funerals, which are usually accompanied by a *dhikr* as well.

After a moment, we hear rhythmic thumping and a muffled *la ilaha illallah* coming from the house next door. The praying men slowly fall into a trance and lose touch with reality. They won't finish until well after midnight. Just in time to get a few hours of sleep before the morning *salah*.

19

RAMZAN IN THE LIFE OF A CHECHEN WOMAN

Ibragim's daughter Kheda has been married twice. She is eighteen years old. Her first husband left her, and she ran away from her second one because he beat her. She fell pregnant, but had an abortion, not wanting to bear his child. She then returned home to her parents.

'He just pulled up! He's here!' she calls excitedly. The phone rings every five minutes. Kheda quickly slips out of the frock she wears around the house. She puts on a tight, sleeveless top and a black, velvet blouse before adding a few golden accessories—wedding gifts from her ex-husbands. She browses through her closet and picks out a narrow, knee-length denim skirt. Like many local girls, Kheda hasn't worn trousers in a while. Ladies' slacks vanished from Chechen markets following a public statement by Ramzan, in which the Chechen president called for women to return to wearing clothing that was more consistent with the republic's 'Chechen and Islamic' traditions. The 'brave women' that buy trousers in neighbouring republics are often met with jeers and taunts from both men and women who share the president's views.

She finishes up her look with strong makeup and high-heeled shoes, and adds a scarf—donned more as a bit of decoration than a piece of Islamic head-gear. The ubiquitous headscarf is another sign of changing attitudes in the republic. An informal presidential order states that women must always wear headscarves in public buildings, schools and universities, in keeping with Chechnya's 'Islamic tradition'. Even the staunchest feminists and non-Muslim women prefer to play it safe and at least carry a scarf in their purses.

'I have a date. Are you coming with me?' Kheda asks. She met Jabrail online, and would see him for the first time that day. Having seen each other only on tiny cellphone pictures, the couple has exchanged text messages, instant messages and phone calls. The time to meet in person has come. Kheda arranged everything ahead of time. She knew that her father would be heading a meeting of the local Sufi fraternity, and would later attend a *dhikr*. Ibragim, concerned about her reputation, doesn't allow her to go out with boys. Her mother is somewhat more understanding.

Jabrail arrived in a car with a friend. He bashfully approached Kheda, greeting her. They set off, walking a few feet away from each other and conversing in Chechen. Normally an enthusiastic teenager, Kheda suddenly turns into a shy, modest and unemotional woman, in accordance with Chechen etiquette. We turned into a side street to keep from drawing attention. They stood off to the side, a few feet apart. Flirting in Chechnya requires space, usually two yards, in order for there to be no doubt about what happened. Holding hands and kissing is out of the question, as are movies, cafés and restaurants, all of which could bring accusations of 'immoral behaviour' upon the girl. Feeling slightly awkward in the role of spying girlfriends, we walked away, occasionally checking if the date was over yet. The rendezvous lasted about forty minutes. 'Why did you keep walking back and forth? You were supposed to stand there and watch us!' Kheda chides us. According to Chechen custom, the girl must be chaperoned by her girlfriends, who observe the date while standing at a distance, so as not disturb them or eavesdrop on them. In case of doubt, the girlfriends can testify to their friend's innocence.

'So how did it go? Did you like him?' I ask.

'Yeah! He's nice and polite—and he wants to get married! But I'm saying no for now. I told him I had to think about it, and that I would get back to him in half a year or so.'

'Why that long? I heard Chechen girls get married quicker.'

'That's true. But you have to do that in the beginning. You can't just say yes right away. I have to refuse three times. Then I'll accept. He suspects that I'm just delaying things, but he can't know for sure.'

'Won't he mind that you've already been married?'

'Oh, that? Well, you know, we have our ways,' says Kheda, blushing. Does she mean the hymen restoration, a highly popular procedure throughout the Caucasus?—I don't dare to ask.

'And besides, we never got married at the town hall. We only had an Islamic wedding.'

It appears that a growing number of young Caucasian couples, even if they aren't particularly religious, are choosing 'trial marriages' and tying the knot in front of a mullah. Is it a compromise between the social taboo against long courtship and the fear of ending up in a dysfunctional marriage? A Caucasian version of cohabitation?

'What if he finds out?' I ask.

'He's not going to find out. He lives in St Petersburg.'

Things don't always work out like that. Although many relationships are sealed over a cellphone or online, 'stalking' remains a popular custom, and can be conducted by the bachelor or his family. The boys friends visit the girl's village or neighbourhood and ask around, talking to her acquaintances, neighbours and teachers to find out how she did at school, if she was well behaved, and—most importantly—how she conducted herself. They will often drop by the girl's home to scrutinise her parents and check their financial status. They observe how she serves guests and whether she is polite and modest. It is not uncommon for the 'stalkers' to ask repeatedly for minor favours or endless cups of tea, noting whether she is patient and obliging. This also gives the girl a chance to show off. If her parents are eager to have the bachelor as their son-in-law, but he isn't quite to her liking, she may serve his mates sloppily, thus signalling her lack of interest in the suitor. One friend, when asked to serve tea, spilled it three times while tripping over every possible piece of furniture. To the mother's great dismay, the plan worked perfectly, and the bachelor never returned.

It would seem that online dating offers Caucasian women a window into the world and may serve as a means for their emancipation, allowing them to make their own decisions. Meanwhile, the only thing that has changed is the medium. News of beautiful maidens in neighbouring villages, once spread via word of mouth, was later replaced by the telephone and the postal service, by which photographs were sent if the bride and groom lived in different cities. Today's medium is mobile Internet. The remaining elements of the matchmaking ritual have undergone minor changes at most. 'Online' brides and grooms employ the similar methods of vetting candidates. Instead of sending their friends to another village, some try to google their partners (although search engines only increase a person's odds of successfully bluffing their way into marriage). Girls still cannot spend time alone with boys, lest their reputations be tarnished; and just as it has been for generations, both sides must ask for their fathers' blessing.

The online dating world has also seen the incursion of parents, who nevertheless remain faithful to the matchmaking tradition. The adults share their children's screennames and social networking profiles, hoping to find a suitable candidate. They use the new medium to arrange marriages for their children, and often reserve banquet halls many months ahead of time—a task that can pose a far greater challenge than the actual search for the bride. One of the stories circulating around in many versions says that one lazy (or trustful) businessman entrusted his parents with the entirety of the wedding preparations, including the search for the wife, and was so pressed for time that he didn't show up until the hour of the ceremony. He had only seen his future wife on pictures emailed to him for approval.

* * *

For now, weddings still take place 'in real life'. The ceremony starts during the day, usually around noon, and lasts until the evening. Poorer families hold the reception in their own courtyards, while the more affluent rent banquet halls or gardens in which tables are arranged and pavilions are erected. The bride must look her best on this day, and wedding dresses are not much different from those found in the West. Under Soviet rule, local tastes in fashion grew visibly similar to European standards. But Ramzan has recently begun voicing his views on this topic as well. In August 2009, the sale of wedding outfits that did not comply with the 'traditional Chechen' style was banned. Only long-sleeved dresses with high necklines and traditional Chechen ornaments were permitted. All other styles were to disappear from shops within one day. Desperate shopkeepers moved their businesses to Daghestani and Ingush markets or searched feverishly for tailors capable of making the necessary adjustments. There's no joking with Ramzan.

During the wedding, the couple are not the centre of attention, especially following a wedding ceremony presided over by a mullah. The bride stands off to the side, and is expected to remain solemn and silent. Often the groom does not participate in the reception at all, observing it instead from a distance, in the company of friends. The revelry and dancing is reserved for the guests, who abstain from drinking at the party, especially now that Islamic norms have begun exerting a greater influence on family life. Dry weddings are a response to Islamic traditions and the demands of the current administration (both of which have been major opponents to the consumption of alcohol). In early 2009, the Chechen government introduced a *sukhoy zakon* (lit. 'dry law'), similar to the one imposed by Gorbachev in the eighties. High-proof alcohol is only sold between eight and ten o'clock in the morning, and mainly in cities (except for Ramadan, when no alcohol is sold at all). Many villages are completely dry. At least officially.

The wedding dance of choice is always the Lezginka, popular in many forms throughout the Caucasus. Chechen music stars are sometimes invited to entertain the guests with popular hits. But, yet again, there is a caveat: according to Ministry of Culture regulations, only songs consistent with the 'Chechen mentality' may be performed at weddings. The contradiction between Chechen and Islamic tradition has led many pious families to invite *nashīd* (chants) groups to perform the traditional Islamic songs at their children's weddings instead.

Newlyweds are also bound by a series of prohibitions. They are not permitted to touch in public places or to have any physical contact at home when in the presence of elders. The groom is separated from his parents-in-law for a certain period, and avoids seeing his own mother and father as well. The bride must never speak first in the presence of men and elders. She must assist her mother-in-law in household chores and serve others. She is also expected to become pregnant as soon as possible.

* * *

Kheda's sister Patimat was married to a mullah from a nearby village at the age of twenty-three. Everything, from courtship, to the wedding, to the divorce, was conducted according to Islamic law. They split up after two years, shortly after the birth of their daughter.

'We didn't mean to get divorced,' she sighs. 'He said "I divorce you" three times in a fit of anger, and later regretted it. But what happened, happened. I have my pride—there was no way I could have gone back to him after that. Especially after everyone found out what had happened.'

Patimat's divorce became the subject of gossip, which was fuelled by the fact that the Chechen television channels happened to be debating the issue of marital problems at the time.

'Kadyrov himself appeared on TV and explained exactly how Muslim marriage and divorce work.'

According to Sharia law, if a man says 'I divorce you' to his wife three times, his words are legally binding and cannot be undone. If the couple decides to get back together, they must first enter into marriage with other people. Only after the subsequent marriage has been dissolved may they once again be married. Should the new, temporary marriage be consummated? No one knows for sure. It is said that a divorced wife would be given to a friend for the wedding night *pro forma*, and the couple would later remarry. This, however, cannot be done overnight. The pair must wait three months and see if a child is conceived in the second marriage (even if both sides swear that their relationship has not been consummated).

The mullah had married again, and Patimat had moved in with her parents. She was happy to have custody over her child (according to Chechen law and Islamic tradition, children are handed over to the father after a divorce, and the mother is granted visitation rights). The mullah would like Patimat to come back to him as his first wife, but she cannot imagine living in a threesome. Who knows what will happen in a few years, should Ramzan succeed in legalising polygamy. Will it be easier to convince Chechen women that a *ménage à trois* is the norm?

* * *

'Chechen Women's Day is coming up in two days,' Kheda announces. Posters have indeed been appearing around town, boasting slogans such as 'The heroic Chechen woman is the bulwark of the nation' and 'Glory to the Chechen woman'. The new holiday was first proclaimed in September 2009, and was likely intended to rival International Women's Day on 8 March, still a popular occasion in Chechnya. 'New Women's Day' was introduced to commemorate the events of 1819, when forty-six Chechen women died while escaping from the *aul* of Dadi-Yurt, which the tsar's army set fire to. The raft on which they were attempting to make their getaway sunk (or, according to a more popular version, was sunk). The women chose to die and keep their virtue rather than fall into the hands of the soldiers.

'They say Ramzan is going to give every woman 5,000 roubles!'[1] says Kheda excitedly.

Her sister chills her enthusiasm. 'They were supposed to give us 5,000 for doctor's day too, and we only got 200.'

'Oh, you know that Ramzan will keep his word. He's an honest man, it's just his administration that's a bunch of crooks. You'll see, he'll give it to us!'

Islam and Ramzan have made clear encroachments into the lives of Chechen families, especially women, to whom most of the new rules apply, and who sit in front of the television set in the evening, enraptured by Ramzan's lectures on Islam and Chechen tradition. There is no shortage of religious and patriotic programming. Even private networks have been urged to educate society in the spirit of Islam and Chechen tradition instead of airing Western movies. Will Ramzan's attempts to discipline women help 'heal' the Chechen nation, lost as it is in post-war chaos? Who knows. It is hard not to laugh when hearing news of yet another seemingly absurd ban, and one would be hard pressed not to view these rules as an attempt to limit the rights of women, most of whom nevertheless interpret Ramzan's newly created traditions as a return to ancient Chechen and Muslim customs, which they are eager to observe (or pretend to observe) in the name of 'moralising' the nation of Chechnya. Perhaps Ramzan's 'Islamopatriotic' message is the first acceptable ideology to appear since the fall of the USSR—one that also answers the question 'how and why should we live?'

Chechen feminists continue to ridicule Ramzan's rules and bans and defy his attempts to discipline them. But they remain the minority, and there is little they can do. For now, all that is left for them is to gather in the privacy of their own homes (in trousers and with bare heads), and raise a glass of champagne on Women's Day.

* * *

'It didn't work out,' Kheda says a half year later when I ask about Jabrail. In the late evening, Kheda is secretly chatting with boys taking care that neither her brothers nor father sees her. She covers her head with the pillow to avoid being heard talking.

Patimat is no longer at home I learn from Kheda.

'Did she come back to her first husband as a second wife?'—I ask.

'A man from Gudermes married her'—says Kheda.

'Oh, how she cried when she was leaving'—Kheda tells me in the evening. 'She didn't like him?'—I ask.

'No, she didn't want to leave her little girl behind.'

'There was no way out of that?'

'No. She knew that she would have to leave her daughter with her first husband. She knew she had no choice. Neither her new nor old husband would agree. Maybe after some time. She knew that her daughter will be unhappy with her step-mother who hates her.'

How surprised I was to see Patimat on Skype a half year later. 'It didn't work out'—she said without concern.

20

NATASHA

It's a rainy September evening. Dusk is falling. Ibragim has just returned from evening prayers at the mosque. He pulls a handful of dates from his pocket and hands them out to the children. It's Ramadan, the Islamic month of fasting, during which Muslims are required to refrain from eating or drinking in the day. They must wait until dusk to break their fast, preferably with dates and water, as was common in the times of the Prophet Muhammad.

We sit down to dinner with Ibragim, for whom it is the first meal of the day. His daughters wait on us, refilling our plates every once in a while with *zhizhig-galnash*, Chechen meat dumplings covered in a thick layer of garlic sauce. Chechen women do not usually sit at the table with men. They eat their meals in the kitchen, or wait until the men have finished before having their dinner.

Ibragim's youngest son sits on the doorstep, gluing tissue paper ornaments on to old flowerpots. The boy likes flowers, and spends his free time tending to them. He listens to our conversation with interest, but says nothing.

'If it weren't for Natasha [Natalya Estemirova], Malik would have been dead,' Ibragim says. Hearing his own name, the boy looks up from his flowers for a moment.

'She would visit us and spend the night. She slept in your room. How could they kill such a good woman ... Those animals.' Ibragim spits in disgust. 'They're going to burn in hell,' he curses under his breath.

* * *

'It was the autumn of 2005,' Ibragim begins. 'A military UAZ[1] pulled up to our house at dawn. They demanded that we open the gate and they threatened to break it down if we didn't let them in. A couple of uniformed Chechen men in ski masks ransacked our house, cursing the whole time.' They forced Malik into the car. His mother and sisters cried, 'He's innocent! Where are you taking him? How can you treat your own people like this?' But their pleas fell on deaf ears. The men shouted at them to stay quiet. That morning Malik disappeared. So did five of his friends from Novye Atagi.

The villagers tried to find an explanation for the arrests. 'Why did they take our boys? Is the village being punished for not being supportive enough of the administration? Maybe we should put up a portrait of Kadyrov [senior] or name a school after him. Or at least a sports club.' Other villages had done just that in the hope of placating the authorities.

By 2005, 'constitutional order' had long been reinstated in Chechnya. The media talked about reconstruction and stabilisation. But while combat operations had ceased, terror was still a part of everyday life in Chechnya. No one knew when the time would come for them or their family. Everyone secretly hoped that the abductions and arrests happened 'for a reason' and could not affect normal, honest people that did not defy the government and who had never held a gun in their hands, or had surrendered their weapons long ago. It was also believed that the Russian military, particularly *kontraktniki*, were behind the events, yet the federal army's campaign of terror was gradually giving way to an internal, Chechen one. The line separating 'them' from 'us' and traitors from heroes was becoming blurred. Traitors became heroes; heroes became terrorists. That was precisely the result Russian authorities were expecting when they began to reframe the Russian–Chechen conflict as a fight between rival Chechen parties (part of a policy known as 'Chechenisation'), which was slowly becoming a reality.

'We were so naïve to believe that the war was over.' says Ibragim, smiling sadly. 'We even submitted a petition to the government—a government we thought was ours, a Chechen government. We wrote, "It would appear that everything is on the right track for stabilisation. We have a government and a president. If that is true, then how long must we live as if we were ruled by warlords?" They probably didn't even read it.'

'So we took to the streets. We demanded the release of the boys,' Ibragim says. 'We blocked a bridge on the road between Grozny and Novye Atagi. They promised to help if we opened the road. But nobody took up the case. They hoped we would give up, but we just blocked the road again. We did it over and over again.'

After a few days, one of the boys was unexpectedly released. He was thrown out of a car outside of Grozny. A passing driver took pity on the beat-up teenager and gave him a ride home. Exhausted and battered, Apti was immediately taken to the hospital. He neither knew where he was nor by whom and for what reason he had been tortured. Why was he the only one let go? Did he have relatives in high places? Or did he manage to prove his relation, however distant, to his torturers? Perhaps his family paid the right person the right amount of money?

The villagers returned to the bridge. Police and *siloviki* (security forces) threatened the protesters, with no result. It was mostly women who participated in the roadblock, knowing that Chechen police would think twice before resorting to the use of force. In the Caucasus, even the slightest act of violence against women is met with serious reprisals on the part of the victim's relatives, and may even lead to the death of the perpetrator. This gave the police no choice but to stand down. (For similar reasons, trade and smuggling across the Russian–Azeri border was commonly the domain of women; men were more likely to be beaten and searched by customs officers and had to pay greater bribes, making the venture unprofitable.)

'The chief administrator even paid me a visit,' laughs Ibragim. 'He begged me to put an end to this *bezpredel* [lawlessness]. It turned out that he had gotten into trouble too. He was abducted and severely beaten by "unidentified assailants" who threatened to kill him if he didn't put an end to the picket on the road.'

'Soon the whole village was in trouble,' Ibragim says, turning serious. 'They came and destroyed our bakery, accusing the owners of baking bread for "Wahhabis". The next day an entire police division showed up at the Friday sermon at our mosque. They demanded that we "take care" of the picketing women and threatened that "soon four more thugs from the village would be arrested and punished without trial".'

Everyone knew perfectly well that the abducted youths had nothing to do with crime of any sort, but they feared their sons could meet the same fate through more abductions and 'Wahhabi' hunts. They knew that the police would keep their word.

* * *

Drawn-out demonstrations and protests are a rarity in Chechnya, and usually end after the first threats. The authorities were thus at a loss as to how to suppress the protest by the women of Novye Atagi. Their steadfast, long-term blockade of the main road was a gesture of bravery and desperation by people living in a world ruled by whomever was strongest, richest and most ruthless. With time, the remaining villagers, fearing retribution, showed waning solidarity with the protesters. It wouldn't be the first instance of *zachistki* in Novye Atagi. Rather than protest openly in such situations, families often quietly raise the money—borrowing from relatives and selling their homes—to buy back the freedom of their loved ones: dead or alive. Multitudes of soldiers made a living from human trafficking during the war. People would pay for anything: to keep their sons or daughters from being raped, killed or maimed. Bodies—dead or alive—became a highly profitable commodity. Initially, only living people were subject to trafficking, but the Russian army eventually realised how important the bodies, or even just the heads, of the dead were to Chechens. A single price was set for both. Chechens were prepared to pay just as much for their dead loved ones in order to bury them with dignity.

* * *

'We had begun to give up hope,' Ibragim continues his story. 'We didn't even know if Malik was alive. I had started thinking about where I was going to get the money. Was my brother abroad well-off enough to help? Should I call my relatives in Moscow? That's when we met Natasha. Thanks to her the media caught wind of the arrest. The television station "Vaynakh" shot a story about us. They ended up getting their tapes confiscated by the police, but more and more people were finding out about the story—journalists, human rights activists. That made the local police uncomfortable. We also found out that the boys were being held on suspicion of murdering a police officer in Atagi. Some of them "confessed" to the crime. What about the ones who didn't crack? Were they still alive? There was a glimmer of hope. We stopped the roadblock and tried to find out what condition the boys were in. We started our own investigation.'

'Malik was released after a year. He was tortured, beaten, electrocuted, and had his nails pulled out in jail. He passed out several times.' Ibragim lowers his voice to keep Malik from overhearing him. It still comes as an embarrassment to a Chechen man to talk about male 'weakness', even in regard to torture. 'He didn't think he would make it out alive. They tortured him so badly that he ended up "confessing". It later turned out that the police officer he was accused of murdering was a relative of ours! How ridiculous!'

'I wanted to fight to have my son cleared of charges, but the police stopped me. "You got your son back, didn't you? So shut up and consider yourself lucky," they said. So I left it at that. There's no winning with them.'

* * *

Abductions, torture and disappearances are an everyday occurrence in today's Chechnya. Such events are usually local in nature and often happen when a 'perpetrator' is urgently needed, or when someone wants to prove their worthiness or take revenge. Some of the victims simply know too much. The spiral of violence continues.

Moscow pays little attention to infighting between local warlords. 'Let them all just kill each other,' seems to be the approach taken by many decision-makers in the capital, who look down on the 'barbaric' and sometimes despised highlanders.

Boys like Malik are victims of a lawless system and an entire network of criminal relationships that take their greatest toll on everyday people; people kidnapped to 'juke' the statistics, to show the chief of police a better clearance rate, and to produce 'terrorists' upon whom to pin murders committed by colleagues. Just arrest a few defenceless boys and torture them into signing false confessions: case closed. The 'perpetrators' are best murdered, just in case. Who needs witnesses?

Thousands of such stories have occurred in Chechnya, and very few resulted in a happy ending. Some, like the one above, were publicised thanks to the efforts of relatives and found their way into reports by Memorial and Amnesty International. Others are told to European civil servants who issue decisions granting refugee status (as evidence of personal persecution), while yet others (or perhaps most) are stored in the memories of loved ones, who remember the cruelty of the police and security forces. Today, only a handful of human rights activists are risking their own lives to save Chechen civilians from the ruthlessness and arbitrariness of the government.

* * *

'Natalia Estemirova. She served society. She was killed by the *siloviki*,' read a sign at a protest—broken up by the police—against the murder of innocent people by the republic's security apparatus.

Natasha Estemirova was a well-known human rights activist in Chechnya, a journalist, an author of a series of exposés on combat operations in Chechnya and winner of numerous awards for her achievements.

She was kidnapped in August 2009 outside her home in Grozny. Her body, bearing signs of torture, was found the next day in the town of Gazi-Yurt in neighbouring Ingushetia. She was fifty years old and left behind a sixteen-year-old daughter.

Natasha Estemirova had repeatedly received death threats. She knew that every minute could be her last. Yet, her search for the truth was too important, and her personal pride too great, to give up on the fight for the lives of innocent people and the proper punishment of criminals. But unlike those whom she investigated, she neither walked around with a retinue of bodyguards, nor drove in an armoured car.

It initially seemed that Kadyrov was behind the murder. Estemirova had made unfavourable comments about the politician, revealing a series of crimes committed by those intimately connected to him. It now appears that the motive behind the killing was much more prosaic. Natasha had simply known too much about a 'local' crime, and intended to go public with the information. The case that Natasha probably lost her life investigating was not much different from the story of the young men from Novye Atagi. A different region, a different police station, different deaths, but similarly ruthless and unpunished criminals, for whom life and human dignity are of little value.

* * *

'I can't believe she's gone,' says Hussein, my lawyer acquaintance when we meet again in Grozny after Natasha's death. 'She had a heart of gold. Everyone liked her and admired her. I still have her text messages. I tried to delete them, but I just couldn't bring myself to do it. I can't let go of them. I sometimes sit and read them ... She made delicious *pierogi*. She promised to invite me over next week ...'

21

ZAREMA

Ramzan stands proudly in front of three corpses. The camera zooms in on the men's mutilated bodies. 'We will not think twice about killing these devils!' Ramzan announces, visibly satisfied with the outcome of the operation. He gestures at the body of a young man. Next to the president stands a pale, middle-aged woman, who we later learn is the boy's mother. She thanks Ramzan for delivering her from the hands of the devil.

* * *

'You'll have to forgive me. We're having Russian food today,' Makka laughs. 'If I had known you were coming, I would have fixed you some Chechen *galushki* [egg noodles].' Her husband nurses a beer in the next room, watching the World Cup on television. The Lezginka playing on the radio fades out, and the news broadcast begins. Makka turns it down. 'I'll leave it on if you're curious how Ramzan's day went,' she jokes. I can hear the quiet mantra coming from the speakers: 'Ramzan Kadyrov visited ...', 'The President of the Chechen Republic Ramzan Kadyrov said ...', 'Ramzan Kadyrov met ...' The Lezginka starts up again.

Makka, a jovial forty-year-old, talks over dinner about her projects, which provide assistance to women who have lost loved ones in the war. She tells us about how much is left to be done in post-war Chechnya, how many people need more than just financial help—they need the help of a psychologist. People are annoyed, she says, that shell-shocked Muscovites were immediately provided with counselling after the March 2010 subway bombings. 'We have bombings and special operations here every day. If anyone needs counselling, it's us,' says Makka. That said, she remains convinced that the situation will one day get better.

'How's Zarema doing? Has she gotten married?' my friend asks Makka, recalling the days when they both worked for the Danish Refugee Council.

'Zarema's gone.' Makka falls quiet, her eyes welling up with tears. She can't bring herself to say a word. Zarema had been a close friend of hers. The two worked together, helping refugees during the war. An uncomfortable silence falls over the room.

'They took her away six months ago, in November 2009. I haven't heard from her since.'

'Who took her? Why? What did she do?'

Zarema, Makka's peer, was a cheerful, chubby woman who worked for the Danish Refugee Council. She spoke English, participated in international projects and spent most of her time at work. Like many young, well-educated Chechen women, Zarema never started a family. By the time they're ready to abandon their careers to work on their personal lives, it is often too late. And, like many women of her generation, Zarema turned to Islam after the war, donning longer dresses and covering her head with a scarf. Many older family members, who had been brought up in Soviet times, disapproved of this new Islamic behaviour. But Zarema was by no means a radical; she kept her views to herself, devoting her life to her job and her faith. She secretly hoped to start a family one day, and had been renovating her bombed-out house in the Leninsky district of Grozny, where she planned to live.

It was the last day of October. Construction workers were pulling a tarp over an unfinished portion of the roof, when security forces drove up to both sides of the house. *Siloviki* piled out of the jeeps and began firing on the neighbouring house. Was someone hiding inside? Was that house the actual target? Or were they just trying to frighten the neighbours into minding their own business? Shots were fired into Zarema's house as well, and the building was soon engulfed in flames. A twenty-year-old man was killed in the operation. Zarema was forced into a car. She has not been seen since. Like any 'respectable' special ops unit, the *siloviki* continued to storm the house until firefighters arrived on the scene and extinguished the blaze. It would be a long time before someone removed the man's charred corpse from the front yard.

On the evening news, residents of Grozny heard about a special operation headed by Ramzan himself; it was a successful operation, like every one reported on TV. According to official accounts, two fighters had been killed.

None of the *siloviki* sustained any casualties. There was no mention of the kidnapped woman.

'Her poor mother is still looking for her. It's been over half a year ...' says Makka. 'She's written thousands of petitions, complaints, and requests. She's even written to Strasbourg.'

We meet Zarema's mother Lida the next day. Despite the hardship she has endured she is a cheerful 'Soviet' woman. Like most of her generation, she was born in Kazakhstan, where the Chechens were deported in 1944. She lived in a Polish–Chechen *kolkhoz*. Lida recalls how her grandmother and her Polish friend would pray together at the Polish and Muslim cemetery, how they would visit each other and how close the two were. Her parents spent the rest of their lives in Kazakhstan. Lida came home to Chechnya, where she found work at the post office. Like many others, she deeply believed in the cause of communism. She was so devoted to her job as a post office accountant that she nearly lost her life during the bombing of Grozny. She was saved by Chechen militants who escorted her (and the post office's money) to a safe place.

'People were different back then, during the first war,' she says. 'Our *boeviki* [fighters] divided everything they earned into three: a third for themselves, a third for the orphans and a third for the disabled. They were honest men. It wasn't until the second war that people started turning into animals. After that, they only thought about themselves. That still hasn't changed. People have grown so jaded.' Lida has many reasons to believe what she says.

* * *

We pass newly renovated neighbourhoods that look as if they were transplanted from a 1950s Central European military base. We drive into Grozny's Leninsky district, into a neighbourhood of red brick single-family homes. Everything looks clean and new (Chechens pride themselves on cleanliness. To this day, guests in some houses will find, upon leaving, that the host has discreetly polished their shoes).

Renovation is under way on every block. The air is heavy with the smell of lime and paint. Construction crews come in from as far as Vietnam and the neighbouring republics, particularly Daghestan, where construction work is regarded as an inferior occupation, unworthy of royalty (from which most Daghestanis claim to descend). But it's a different matter when the job is in another republic, where no one can see them, and the pay isn't bad. They build mansions with arcades and modest, square houses with outdoor kitchens, small courtyards and tall gates. Some houses, bombed out and collapsed, will never be renovated, and are hidden behind high fences. Their owners are unlikely to ever return from their homes in the calm and cosy suburbs of Oslo and Vienna.

Lida opens the gate. We enter the courtyard. We see the charred ruins of a house. The plastic window frames have melted into shapeless puddles. Broken pieces of broad, red roof shingles hang off the burnt rafters. Parts of the house are taped off for safety. Unused bricks and bags of lime are piled in the corner. Anything of value has been looted long ago. The old, unburnt part of the house contains a cabinet with last year's preserves. A braid of garlic hangs by the refrigerator. Zarema would occasionally spend the night here with a friend, supervising the renovation of her future home.

'This is where they took away my daughter,' Lida says, tears streaming down her cheeks. 'I'd retract everything, even the petition to Strasbourg, if I could just see my little Zarema! I've begged the president of Ingushetia on my knees, I raised money from family members. I know that Zarema is still alive! They couldn't have just taken her for no reason!' She says she once met a woman on the street who claimed to have seen Zarema in prison. Lida has seen several fortune tellers. All of them maintain that Zarema is still alive. Lida continues to visit them in secret, ever since Ramzan banned the services of psychics and fortune tellers, claiming them to be 'un-Islamic'. The reason behind the decision might be that such people, having talked to many a grieving mother, simply know too much.

* * *

Why was Zarema taken away? Was it a mistake? Maybe she just knew too much? Or perhaps she lent assistance to a boy who turned out to be a *boevik* (or was posthumously declared to have been one)? The neighbours refuse to talk about it. They saw Zarema's kidnappers speeding away in a jeep. They know she was taken away by the Kadyrovites. But the neighbours refuse to testify; after all, the operation was led by Kadyrov himself.

'It wouldn't do any good, anyway,' they say. 'You understand, don't you? I have a family, I want to live.'

The Danish Refugee Council remains neutral on the issue. As a humanitarian relief organisation, the DRC 'doesn't do politics'. They refuse to send an official letter to the government. The organisation prefers to mind its own business; it risks losing its office in Grozny, its projects would fail and funding would fall through. Zarema's co-workers avoid the topic.

'I feel bad for the girl, but she must have had something on her conscience. Maybe she was cohabiting with a *boevik*? Maybe she was hiding him?'

'Zarema wanted to start a family so much. Maybe she fell in love with him?' another co-worker offers uncertainly.

'They say she started getting into Wahhabism,' another woman adds, as if to reassure her own conscience. The everyday propaganda of Chechen television is reaping rewards, affecting how people speak and think about kidnappings, disappearances and torture.

Although military operations in Chechnya ostensibly ceased a few years ago, silent terror continues to claim victims—victims like Zarema. They disappear without a trace, murdered, left to die in jail cells. Many are posthumously 'declared' to have been *boeviki*. Ramzan's fight against 'the devils among us' is winning over growing numbers of Chechens. Seeing the relative peace he has brought to the streets makes them all the more likely to believe him. They are prepared to accept any ruler, as long as he keeps a new war from breaking out. They are easily dazzled with fountains and new buildings, and are genuinely thankful to Ramzan for quickly rebuilding the republic, for the schools and the hospitals. They are prepared to forget about the deaths of their friends, co-workers and loved ones. They have chosen to cooperate, and have become obedient—by choice or by force. Having grown weary of warfare, they shut out the tragedies of others (at least until their own families are hurt), rationalising the actions of the government. Order requires sacrifice.

* * *

Lida changes her phone number every two months. She often stays away from home. She knows that somebody may give her away anytime. She has already been threatened. The Chechen authorities hate it when people write petitions to Strasbourg. They can arrest her anytime. Lida warns us not to be around for too long. She worries about us. There are informers everywhere.

* * *

We leave Makka's flat. I catch a glimpse of a gun in a back pocket of a young guy standing in front of the building. All of a sudden I stiffen and stop. 'What's wrong?'—Makka asks. I realise that after a couple of weeks in Chechnya it is ridiculous to panic at the mere sight of a gun—a common 'male' attribute in these parts along with the fancy mobile phones.

'Don't worry'—she says. 'It happens to us too. Especially if we stay away from the country for a while. This is why some of us never come back".

* * *

Speaking of Chechnya's future, Ramzan smiles in front of the cameras. He speaks about boosting the tourism business. He is about to start the reconstruction of a tourist base at the Kazenoi-Am mountain lake at the border with Daghestan. He wants to build hotels and ski resorts.

Who knows, maybe in a couple of years backpackers will make it to Chechnya. They would take photos of the fountains and mosques of Grozny, enjoy themselves at the lake and in the hot springs near Gudermes. They will be safe. Just like the rare visitors to the Soviet Union. Sightseeing in Moscow and Leningrad, they were isolated from Soviet people's miseries and have not heard of people being placed in jails or sent to Siberia. Like Zarema, they passed away quietly.

NOTES

Some names have been changed for the sake of the security of the informants.

1. ATHEISTS IN THE MOUNTAINS

1. State Automobile Inspectorate (Государственная Автомобильная Инспекция)

2. THE BEEKEEPER-PHILOSOPHER

1. The Arabic transcription system used for local languages.
2. In Persian: "hidden from sight", supernatural creatures in Islamic mythology. Further explained in Chapter 4.

3. 'WAHHABIS'

1. Fur hat usually made of karakul sheep skin.

4. MAALI

1. *Gidro-electro-stancya.*
2. Administrative centre of the district.
3. Free citizens.
4. A Turkic word that traditionally denotes a skillful equestrian. These days it can be used for any young man in the Caucasus or Central Asia.
5. Old Believers (*starovyery*) refused to accept the liturgical reforms introduced by patriarch Nikon and separated from the Russian Orthodox Church after 1666. In the subsequent years they split into a number of different sects/denominations that spread around the world.
6. Хатан-Бугоб-Ккал.

6. JIHAD

1. *Kontrterroristicheskaya operatia*—counterterrorist operation.

2. A book by Aleksandr Solzhenitsyn about the Soviet forced labour camp system. It was first published in 1973 in Paris.

7. SHAMIL'S SIBERIA

1. Administrative province in Russia located in the Southern Federal District.
2. Polish TV show, popular also in the Soviet Union.

8. SHEIKHS

1. Polish brand of bison grass vodka.
2. A string of prayer beads, also known as *tespih* (Turkish). In Russian it is called *chiotki*.
3. An Arabic term for spiritual practice embodied in a Sufi order.
4. City in the south of Daghestan.
5. According to Qur'an *sadaqah* is a voluntary contribution and can take the form of a good deed, material or financial assistance, or even just a smile. Giving *sadaqah* pleases God and can purify the soul of its sins.
6. Abdulla is believed to have lived up to 115 years and was buried in Derbent in the late nineties.

9. URAZA BAYRAM

1. *Gidro-electro-stancya*—hydroelectric power plant.
2. Charity given out at the end of fasting.
3. For more on concepts of purity and dirt, see Mary Douglas, *Purity and Danger: An Analysis of Concepts of Pollution and Taboo*, London: Routledge and Keegan Paul, 1966.

10. ABDURAKHMAN

1. A Polish brand of bison grass vodka.
2. The 1991 coup d'état attempt (August Putsch) was led by a group of hard-line members of Soviet Union's government with an intention to turn down the Soviet president Mikhail Gorbachev. The coup collapsed in two days, but it had nevertheless destabilised the Soviet Union.
3. The government building in Moscow, also known as the Russian White House.
4. Makhachev died in a car accident near Moscow in 2013.

11. SAUNAS

1. The virtual Islamic state proclaimed in the autumn of 2007 by the Islamist militant leader Dokka Umarov.
2. Many Daghestanis were repatriated from Central Asia, Georgia and Azerbaijan following the collapse of the Soviet Union.

12. IF I EVER WERE A SULTAN

1. Orginal title: Кавказская пленница (Kavkazkaya plennica).

15. THE MERCENARY

1. As of September 2015, this was equivalent to 53 US dollars.
2. Communal apartment.
3. Восстановление конституционного порядка.
4. Борьба с международным терроризмом.

16. THE SHAHIDS

1. A Central Asian prison (from the Persian *zindân*). In the North Caucasus the word *zindan* was to describe a dungeon, or hole in the ground used both to keep the captives and as a shelter from bombs.

18. THE PILGRIMAGE

1. A dagger.
2. The representative of many other nations have been sent to Kazakhstan: Chechen and Ingush, Tatars, Bulgars, Greeks, Karachai, Balkars.

19. RAMZAN IN THE LIFE OF A CHECHEN WOMAN

1. As of September 2015, this was equivalent to 75 USD.

20. NATASHA

1. UAZ-469, a military vechicle widely used in the former USSR, produced by an automobile manufacturer (*Ulyanovsky Avtomobilny Zavod*) based in the city of Ulyanovsk.

BIBLIOGRAPHY

Abdullaev, Magomed, *Sufizm i yego raznovidnosti na severo-vostochnom Kavkaze*, Makhachkala: Noviy den, 2000.

Babchenko, Arkady, *One Soldier's War in Chechnya*, London: Portobello, 2008.

Belozorov, Vitaly, *Etnicheskaya karta Severnogo Kavkaza*, Moscow: OGI, 2005.

Bobrovnikov, Vladimir, *Abreki na Severnom Kavkaze*, Moscow: OGI, 2001.

—— *Musulmanie Severnogo Kavkaza*, Vostochnaya literature, Moscow: RAN, 2002.

—— *Shariatskiye sudy na Severnom Kavkaze*, Moscow: Otechestvennye zapiski N 5, 2003.

Chesnov, Yan, 'Trudno bit' chechencem: Teypy, ikh rol' v proshlom i nastoyashchem', *Nezavisimaya Gazeta*, 22 Sep. 1994.

Ciesielski, Stanisław, *Rosja-Czeczenia: Dwa stulecia konfliktu*, Wrocław: Wydawnictwo Uniwersytetu Wrocławskiego, 2003.

Crews, Robert, *For Prophet and Tsar: Islam and Empire in Russia and Central Asia*, Cambridge, MA, and London: Harvard University Press, 2006.

Derluguian, Georgi, 'The Forgotten Complexities of Jihad in the North Caucasus', in Lale Yalcin-Heckmann and Bruce Grant (eds), *Caucasus Paradigms: Anthropologies, Histories, and the Making of a World Area*, Münster: LIT Verlag, 2008.

Evangelista, Matthew, *The Chechen Wars*, Washington, DC: Brookings Institution Press, 2002.

Falkowski, Maciej and Mariusz Marszewski, *The 'Tribal Areas' of the Caucasus: The North Caucasus—An Enklave of 'Alien Civilization' within the Russian Federation*, Warsaw: OSW Studies, 2010.

Forsyth, James, *The Caucasus: A History*, Cambridge: Cambridge University Press, 2013.

Gamzatov, Rasul, *Mój Dagestan*, trans. Jerzy Jędrzejewicz, Warsaw: Państwowy Instytut Wydawniczy, 1971.

Gralewski, Mateusz, *Kaukaz. Wspomnienia z 12-letniej niewoli: Opisanie kraju— ludność—zwyczaje i obyczaje*, Lviv: Księgarnia Polska, 1877.

Kalinowski, Karol, *Pamiętnik mojej żołnierki na Kaukazie i niewoli u Szamila od roku 1844 do 1854*, Warsaw: Wydawnictwo W. Dawida, 1883.

Karpov, Yuri, *Zhenskoe prostranstvo v kulturie narodov Kavkaza*, St Petersburg: Petersburskoe Vostokovedene, 2001.

Khasiev, Said-Magomed, 'O cennostnoy shkale chechencev', *Lam*, 4, 2002.

Kisriev, Enver, *Islam i vlast' v Dagestanie*, Moscow: OGI, 2004.

Lieven, Anatol, *Chechnya: Tombstone of Russian Power*, New Haven: Yale University Press, 1998.

Lokshina, Tatiana (ed.), *Chechnya, zhizn' na voyne*, Moscow: DEMOS, 2007.

Malashenko, Alexey, *Islamskiye oriyentiry Severnogo Kavkaza*, Moscow: Moskovskiy Centr Carnegie, 2001.

—— *Ramzan Kadyrov: rossiyskiy politik kavkazskoy nacional'nosti*, Moscow: Moskovskiy Centr Carnegie, 2009.

Malashenko, Alexey and Dmitry Trenin, *Vremia Yuga*, Moscow: Moskovskiy Centr Carnegie, 2002.

Politkovskaya, Anna, *A Dirty War: A Russian Reporter in Chechnya*, London: Harvill Press, 2001.

—— *A Small Corner of Hell: Dispatches from Chechnya*, Chicago: University of Chicago Press, 2003.

Prozorov, Stanislav, *Islam na territorii bivshey Rossiyskoy Imperii: enciklopedicheskiy slovar*, Vostochnaya literatura, Moscow: RAN, 1998.

Quran, trans. Jan Bielawski, Warsaw: Państwowy Instytut Wydawniczy, 1986.

Rasulov, Yasin, 'Jihad na Severnom Kavkaze: storonniki i protivniki', online at http://www.kavkazcenter.com/russ/islam/jihad_in_ncaucasus

Rechkalov, Vadim, *Zhivih smertnic ne bivaet. Chechenskaya knizhka*, Moscow: Vremya, 2005.

Sadulaev, German, *Ya chechenec*, Yekaterinburg: Ultra. Kultura, 2006.

Seierstad, Asne, *The Angel of Grozny: Inside Chechnya*, London: Virago, 2008.

Smith, Sebastian, *Allah's Mountains: The Battle for Chechnya*, London: I.B. Tauris, 2009.

Tishkov, Valery, *Chechnya: Life in a War-Torn Society*, London: Harvill Press, 2001.

Waal, Thomas de, *The Caucasus: An Introduction*, Oxford: Oxford University Press, 2010.

Ware, Robert B., *Dagestan: Russian Hegemony and Islamic Resistance in the North Caucasus*, New York, 2010.

Yarlykapov, Akhmet, 'Narodnyy islam i molodezh' Severo-Zapadnogo Kavkaza', *Etnograficheskoe obozrene*, 2 (2006).

Yuval-Davis, Nira, *Gender and Nation*, London: SAGE, 1997.

INDEX

40, 42, 113, 116, 119, 126, 155;
suppression of rebellion in
Buynaksk, 40, 41–2; kidnapping
of PAN professors in Daghestan,
19; Kvanada placed on list of
bombing targets, 69

2000 Khava Barayeva suicide bombs
army base in Chechnya, 121

2001 Aiza Gazuyeva assassinates
Gaidar Gadzhiyev with suicide
bomb, 121

2002 assassination of Khattab, 134;
Moscow theatre hostage crisis,
121–2

2003 Tushino bombing, 121;
assassination of Nadirshakh
Khachilayev, 106; Akhmad
Kadyrov appointed president of
Chechnya, 126

2004 assassination of Akhmad
Kadyrov, 126; Beslan school siege,
121–2

2006 publication of *Islam in the
Former Russian Empire*, 22

2007 Alu Alkhanov dismissed;
Ramzan Kadyrov appointed
president of Chechnya, 125, 126

2008 Dmitry Medvedev inaugurated
president, 49–50

2009 end of anti-terror operations in
Chechnya; suicide bombings
resume, 117, 118, 122, 124, 132;
Grozny airport granted international status, 128

2010 Moscow Metro bombings, 153

2013 Said Amirov arrested and
imprisoned, 82

2015 assassination of Boris Nemtsov,
viii

Saakashvili, Mikheil, 49

sacrifices, 15, 71
sadaqah, 60, 64
Sadulaev, German, 98
Said Efendi, 57–60, 62, 65, 66
Salafism, 22, 23, 24, 28, 32, 40, 61, 69,
70, 89
salah (prayer), viii, 8, 22, 24, 30, 35, 36,
50, 52, 53, 70, 73, 89, 101, 102, 106,
107, 138, 147
Samarkand, Uzbekistan, 75
Samashki, Chechnya, 117
Saudi Arabia, 22, 41, 69, 104, 128
saunas, 28, 77, 86–9, 105
Schengen Area, 83
Second Chechen War (1999–2000), 5,
6, 40, 42, 113, 116, 119, 126, 155
Second World War (1939–45), 115,
126, 136
Senegal, 61
Serzhen'-Yurt, Chechnya, 132, 134
sex, sexuality, vii, 47, 62, 68, 70, 85–9,
91–4, 95–9
adultery, 93, 95–9
birth control, 98
homosexuality, 85, 95
and modest dress, 29, 42, 52–3, 59,
62, 85, 87, 89, 101, 117, 131, 139,
154
pregnancy, abortion, 78, 91, 98, 139,
143–4
promiscuity, 62, 85–9, 95–9, 106
prostitution, 47, 85–9, 94
sexually transmitted diseases
(STDs), 98
tuda-siuda, 95–9
virginity, 96, 98–9, 140
Shadhili Order, 61
Shahada, 37
shahid (martyrs), 44, 46, 103, 104,
117–24
Shali, Chechnya, 122, 132, 135